"Based on your political viewpoint, you are probably drawn to one of two cable news networks that are so polar opposite from each other there is little hope they would ever come together in agreement (let alone unity). Has this same concept entered the church? Is there an ever widening divisiveness among Christians over who is right or wrong? Are brothers and sisters in Christ severing relationships based on differing opinions of individual experiences with God? Dave Wernli's book is superb and timely, providing wonderfully told stories based on scripture and personal experiences. A must read that uncovers a scheme of the enemy to divide the church, and a wealth of anecdotes that provide encouragement to Christians to find a much needed balance in our viewpoint."
—*Rev. Michael Hancock, Senior Pastor, Stafford Foursquare Church (ICFG), Divisional Superintendent, Potomac River Division (ICFG) President/Executive Director, Stafford Hope Center Inc.*

"Dave Wernli has brought much-needed balance to the awareness that our interaction with the living God must have both intellectual and emotional components if it is to be healthy. That dynamic can present great challenges for individuals and churches who often want to go to one extreme or the other. In *Mixed Emotions,* Dave has tackled a difficult subject with winsome wit and wisdom. I found many fascinating tidbits in this book and absolutely loved his illustration concerning 'knowing swings'! This is a thought-provoking and enjoyable read!"
—*Rev Jim Bethany, Senior Pastor, Richland Baptist Church, Founder and President, The Church Unchained: LukeNine1&2 Ministries*

"'Let all things be done decently and in order.' So was Paul's counsel to the rambunctious Corinthians who apparently had no lack of emotional experiences! However, it was not their emotionalism that Paul was primarily addressing but rather their lack of love. *Mixed Emotions* wisely guides us through the minefield of our emotional response to spiritual experiences in our pursuit of God to a well-balanced, thoroughly readable and eminently biblical discussion of people's seemingly 'disorderly' encounters with the Living God. Thank you, Dave, for your timely book! May it bring healing to many who have struggled to rightly steward their heart responses to God's touch."
—*Rev Bowie Curry, Associate Director of the Fredericksburg Prayer Furnace (House of Prayer)*

"Dave Wernli's writing is straightforward and very thought provoking. *Mixed Emotions* will challenge how you approach an experience with God."
—*Colleen Geyer, Coordinator, The County Connector: Stafford's Spiritual Source of Connection*

"Dave brings a well balanced perspective to what could be a difficult subject. This book gently leads you to evaluate the questions, 'Do I know Him? Do I experience Him?' As Dave says, 'It was experiencing His presence, finally meeting Him and knowing Him that changed their lives forever.'"
—*Denise Swett, Executive Director, Fredericksburg Pregnancy Center*

Mixed Emotions

Bringing Balance to the Experience of God's Presence

Dave Wernli

Mobile, Alabama

Mixed Emotions
by Dave Wernli
Copyright ©2014 by Dave Wernli

All rights reserved. This book is protected under the copyright laws of the United States of America. This book may not be copied or reprinted for commercial gain or profit.

Unless otherwise indicated, Scripture is taken from the Holy Bible, NEW INTERNATIONAL VERSION®. Copyright © 1973, 1978, 1984 by Biblica, Inc. All rights reserved worldwide. Used by permission.

Scripture marked NKJV is taken from the New King James Version®. Copyright © 1982 by Thomas Nelson, Inc. Used by permission. All rights reserved.

Scripture marked NAS is taken from the *New American Standard Bible*, Copyright ©1960, 1962, 1963, 1968, 1971, 1973, 1975, 1977 by The Lockman Foundation.

ISBN 978-1-58169-546-5
For Worldwide Distribution
Printed in the U.S.A.

Evergreen Press
P.O. Box 191540 • Mobile, AL 36619
800-367-8203

*To Three Generations of Women
Who Inspire My Life:*

*My mother, Shirley Wernli,
Who first taught me to pursue my
imagination and dreams.*

*My daughter, Vicki Wernli,
It is my pleasure to see you swing
with the Lord. He pushes you now.
Maybe when I am old I can still
give you a push with my walker.*

*And especially to my lovely wife,
Janet Wernli,
I could not be who God's calling me
to be without your partnership.
Here's to the adventure!*

Contents

Introduction xi

1. Reality of Experience 1
2. The Spiritual Realm 13
3. Common Objections 27
4. Practical Discernment 39
5. Experience Leads 54
6. Close Encounters 68
7. Incomplete Experience 82
8. God's Eminent Domain 94
9. A Pride Response 103
10. Down the Mountain 113
11. A Humble Response 126
12. Really Knowing 136

Acknowledgments

Thank you to the all the good people at Evergreen Press who made this book a reality, especially Brian Banashak, Jeff Banashak, and Kathy Banashak.

And a special thank you to Keith Carroll. Without your input this book would never have made it off the ground.

Introduction

Christianity is full of minor controversies that we turn into major ones. Pick one. What is your favorite? But first think about this—of all these controversies that *we* think are so important, what did *Jesus* say was important?

In the parable of the sheep and the goats (Matthew 25:31-46), did Jesus separate the sheep from the goats based on whether they correctly figured out a controversial point of doctrine? No. It was based on whether they manifested God's heart for the poor in their lives. Or how about the parable of the talents (Matthew 25:14-30)? Were the servants rewarded (or chastised) because they got a teaching right (or wrong), or because they lived their lives using the giftings God gave them (or not)?

On that great and terrible day of the Lord (Joel 2:31), when we finally meet Jesus face to face, does anyone really think Jesus is going to ask us, "I know you didn't give squat about the poor, and you never believed or walked in the calling I put on your life, and you never made any attempt to share your faith with anyone, and you never had much of a relationship with Me, but you did correctly understand that controversial topic, right?" Really? If the essence of our Christianity is about having perfect doctrine, about having correctly figured out whatever controversial issue we feel is so important, are we not much more likely to hear Jesus say, "I never knew you. Away from me, you evildoers" (Matthew 7:23)?

I'm not saying that controversial minor points of doctrine are unimportant or should be ignored. Paul, when writing about them (he calls them "disputable matters"), says in

Romans 14:5, "Each one should be fully convinced in his own mind." So it's okay to have strong opinions about these things.

But what I am saying is they are not worth splitting your church over, leaving your church over, or even being upset over. If we cannot worship next to someone whose mind is made up differently than ours about some minor issues, then we have identified ourselves as a Pharisee and need to repent of our pride and self-righteousness.

This book was written to address one of these divisive points of doctrine—our emotional experiences with God. I wrote it not because I think the resolution of this issue is so critical to Christianity, but because I'm tired of watching Christians, brothers and sisters for whom Christ died, tear each other apart over it.

Within Christendom there are two extremes when it comes to this issue. One extreme is that emotional experiences with God are wonderful, even indescribable. They are the be-all, end-all, of Christianity. We just need to get more people to a place where they can experience God and then stay in that place as long as possible. Emotional experiences with God are to be pursued above all else. In fact, an emotional experience is so necessary you may not really be saved if you haven't had one.

To this viewpoint, I say, well, yes and no.

The other extreme is that emotional experiences are at best irrelevant and at worst damaging or even demonic. They are disruptive and certainly have no place in a church service. These experiences are simply manipulation and we should not participate in them. Many Christian leaders who practice them also have shoddy doctrine. The important thing isn't what experience you've supposedly had with God, but how well you know your Bible and how often you read it.

To this viewpoint, I say, well, yes and no.

I think both points of view are right in some areas and wrong in others. We need to find a healthy balance to this issue. I don't think, as so many seem to, that an acceptance of and a caution about emotional experiences are necessarily contradictory. We will discover that emotional experiences are very important, not for salvation, but for knowing the fullness of all God has for us. But an experience is not an end in itself—it has to be stewarded rightly. The bottom line is, is it God or not, and if so, what's He doing in this?

I pray God speaks to everyone who reads this book. I pray it quells controversy rather than raises it. "May the words of my mouth and the meditation of my heart be pleasing in your sight, O Lord" (Psalm 19:14).

Happy reading, and may you be blessed by what you read.

1

Reality of Experience

"Higher, Daddy, higher!" says the curly-haired girl on the swing. I know every one of those brown curls. She is my daughter, and even at five years old, she's a challenge to keep up with. Unlike her older brother who, like me, hangs back and analyzes the situation first, Vicki charges in with both feet. She is my daredevil. I can't push her any higher—the swing is already sweeping out a 180-degree arc.

Vicki doesn't know anything about swings. I know everything about swings. I'm the engineer who has worked in the physical sciences for decades. I can derive their angular momentum, velocity, moment of inertia, and centrifugal force. I can tell you all about the arc of the curve the swing sweeps out on each pass through space. I can even tell you why and how much the motion lessens with each pass unless you add energy to the system with a push. And yet, none of this knowledge makes me smile when I think of a swing.

But Vicki knows swings. They are her favorite thing. In. The. World. She thinks they are only the "funnest" thing ever—the feeling of going higher and higher than the sky and the wind rushing by you, the thrill of flying and the butterflies in your stomach when you start to go backwards, and the excitement and the fright as you're looking straight down at the ground! Was there ever anything better than a swing? What she knows makes her smile every single time she thinks of a swing.

I don't know swings at all.

Why does my little daughter Vicki know swings so much better than I do—the engineer who knows all about them? Because she's the one who has experienced the swing. Experience is how we know reality. Whether it's a swing, skiing, scuba diving, loneliness, or love, we can't say we really know something that we haven't experienced.

Math teachers know that you can sit and listen to them explain fractions, for example, forever. It might even make sense. But you won't actually learn or know fractions until you sit down and actually start doing some problems. Once we experience fractions by doing some problems on our own, then the teacher's lecture begins to make more sense. Experience is how we know reality. This is true in all areas of life: the physical realm, the emotional realm, and even in the spiritual realm.

The Physical Realm

We have five senses through which we experience the reality of the physical world around us. We cannot understand or know something we have not experienced with our senses as deeply as something we have. There are a myriad of examples that illustrate that we can't know the reality of something until we've experienced it. Here are but a few.

Swings & Roller Coasters. Let's talk more about how my little daredevil daughter and I experience swings differently. The scientist in me can tell you all about the swing. I can compute the angular momentum and the velocity at any point in the arc. I know the physical restrictions of how high you can safely go. I know all about swings. But I don't know swings.

My daughter, on the other hand, who knows nothing about physics but actually rides the swing—she knows the swing. She's experienced it. Get the point?

Or think of a new roller coaster in an amusement park. When the owners of the park want to know if the ride is a hit or not, who will they ask? Who knows the reality of the roller coaster better—the PhD physicist who designed it but has never ridden it or the ten-year-old kid who just got off? They will ask the person who knows it the best—the ten-year-old kid! He's experienced it! Was it fun? Does he want to go on it again?

Thunderheads. We all learned in grade school that the tops of cumulous clouds (or thunderheads) are white. We've seen them in books, in movies, and on TV. We all know what they look like. But I personally didn't know how really white and big and cottony and cavernous they were until I took my first airplane ride through one.

Then I had a whole new appreciation for thunderheads. I could see them in the sky and remember my ride through them—how scary and how awesome and how thrilling it was to see something only birds and God had seen until the last century. Although I knew all about them, I didn't really know the reality of what a thunderhead was like until I experienced a thunderhead first hand. TV doesn't do them justice; it's different when you're actually there.

Colors. Think of a blind man trying to understand colors, never having seen (experienced) them. He may know that the color blue is at a frequency of 635 terahertz (THz) in the visual spectrum, while the color red is at 433 THz. He may also know the wavelength of the color blue is 474 nanometers (nm), while a red wavelength is 700 nm. But he doesn't know red or blue, since he can't experience them.

I once saw an episode of the TV show *Simon and Simon* where a man (played by actor Gerald McRaney) was trying to show a blind women colors. He held her hand close to a burning candle, and she pulled it away saying, "Hot!" He said, "Red." But the flame was actually yellow. He had her feel a fuzzy sweater, and she said, "Soft." He said, "Blue." But the sweater was actually green. While he was being very sensitive and clever, he could only help her understand the emotions or images or moods we associate with colors—the "trappings" of colors, if you will. He could not actually teach her to know colors because she was physically incapable of experiencing them.

I have never asked a blind person about fireworks, but somehow I just don't think the blind would find a fireworks display nearly as impressive as the rest of us do. To the blind, fireworks would be indistinguishable from a military naval firing exercise. "What's the big deal? It's just a bunch of bangs!" When a blind man hears the boom of an exploding firework in the sky, he has no way of knowing whether it was red, blue, yellow, green, orange, or white. He doesn't know what color the firework is because he can't see it, let alone what shape or pattern it made in the sky. He doesn't know the reality of what a firework really is, because he can't experience it.

A Limited Window

Our five senses are our window into physical reality, but they are just a window. For instance, looking through the nearest window from where you're reading this book right now to the outside world, there is much more to "outside" than you can see out your window. Even if you're reading this book outside, there is more to outside than you can see all at once. Of the outside world within our visual range, we can only see less than half of it (<180 degrees) at a time. Likewise, there is much more to the physical realm than we can experience with our limited five senses.

Light and sound are actually both just energy vibrating at certain frequencies. The frequency band from 400 to 790 THz we call visible light and experience with our eyes. The frequency band from 15 Hz to 20 KHz we call sound and experience with our ears. But what about the other frequency bands? They are just as real even though we can't directly experience them. We make radios to collect energy at different frequencies, frequencies we cannot experience, and convert it to frequencies we can. We can see the effect of X-rays on film, so we know they are real, but cannot experience them directly.

Before Anton van Leeuwenhoek (a Christian biologist and the father of modern-day microbiology) improved the microscope enough to actually see germs in the 1670s, many reputable scientists did not believe in them. "What? Little beasties we can't see, floating around everywhere in the air? Yeah, right!" Although everyone had experienced or known the effect of germs (everyone had been sick at some time), the human race did not know germs until the microscope extended our sense of sight, and we could actually experience them with our eyes. Then no one could doubt their existence—anyone with a microscope could experience them for himself.

But seeing the germs didn't make them real. They were just as real before we could see them. Seeing them just made them real to us.

So even in the physical realm, there is much to reality we cannot experience, and hence, we cannot really know. We can know about a lot of it through science and with the aid of technology, but there is more to physical reality than we can experience or know. The small piece we actually do know is only known through our experience of it, via our five senses.

A Diverse Window

A common problem for CSI types (Crime Scene Investigators) is that eye witnesses seeing the same event at the same time and even from the same location or angle can have vastly different descriptions of it. Our experiences are personal. No two will be alike from person to person, just like no two people are alike.

But this is okay and does not generally create a problem for us. No one says, "I'm not getting on the roller coaster because everyone else will be sitting in a different seat and so will have a different experience from me."

I grew up in Canyon Country, California, near an amusement park called Magic Mountain. They had one of the first, if not the first, roller coasters in the country with a vertical, 360-degree loop. It was hot stuff in the seventies and called the Revolution.

There were different experiences for different people riding the same coaster. If you looked straight ahead as you went into the loop, the centrifugal force jammed your head down into your chest, so you got a nice view of your lap during the loop. You couldn't move it until you finished the loop. While your lap was not the thrill you rode the coaster to see, it was kind of wild having your chin jammed between your nipples and being unable to move.

On the other hand, some of the veteran riders would look to the side while going down the hill into the loop, so that when your ear got pulled toward your belly, your head would stay sideways. Then you got to see the much more visually stunning view of the horizon turning upside down and back again.

I don't know about you, but if somebody said, "I'm not getting on this ride until everyone agrees to turn their head the same way at the same time so we all have the same experience!" I'd say, "See you when we get off, dude!"

Just because things are different or individualized doesn't mean they're bad, and in the physical and emotional realms we all know this intrinsically.

A Flawed Window

Anyone who has seen a magician knows our five senses are not perfect. If the magician can get us to look in the wrong place at the right time, he can get away with murder.

Literally. Ever see the "woman-sawed-in-half" trick? You saw it happen, but you know it really didn't. Or you saw the magician put the coin in his hand, watched his hand the whole time, and then suddenly the coin disappeared. Did you really see what you thought you saw? Apparently not.

Both kids and adults find optical illusions fascinating. You've probably seen "heat waves" rising from a hot road in the distance appear to be water, like a mirage. But when you get to that spot on the road, it's dry as a bone.

Ever see a spoon "break" as you put it into a glass of water, and the water refracts, or bends, the light? The part in the water and the part out of the water look like they're not even touching, let alone are the same piece of silverware. But in reality they are the same piece of silverware and in fact are in a straight line.

The sound of a train whistle does not really change frequency as it goes by you. But it sure sounds like it does due to the Doppler effect. In reality, however, the sound emitted from the whistle was at a constant frequency.

Our five senses, as good as they are, can be tricked. So they are not necessarily always an accurate picture of even the small bit of physical reality we can experience. What then? Do we make sure we never ever see or hear anything because what we see and hear might be false? Of course not. Our senses are all we've got, so we're stuck using them. What do we do? We train ourselves to distinguish, or discern, between true and false sensory perceptions.

A Risky Window

For some experiences, it's the fact that they involve an element of danger or risk that makes them worthwhile. Take skydiving, for example. While I myself would never jump out of a perfectly good airplane, those who do say it's an indescribable thrilling time. I can't understand it because I've never experienced it. I can't know what it's like.

Every parent wants his or her child to experience life. There are times, although certainly not all the time, when a parent has to let his or her child experience the consequences of his or her foolish behavior or choice of friends. We all know over-protective parents who try to keep their children safe, literally to a fault, by keeping them inside the equivalent of a rubber room—not letting them play sports, ride a bike, or do anything else where they might get hurt. And we all feel sorry for those kids.

Experience is risky, but it's well worth it. A line from the movie *The Princess Diaries* is, "The brave may not live long, but the cautious do not live at all." Making sure none of our experiences contain any element of risk would be to not live at all, not to mention not living life to its fullest. The only truly safe place in this world is the inside of a casket. Think about that.

The Emotional Realm

As Christians, we know there is much more to reality than the physical realm. Actually, every human being knows and believes this, whether he or she admits it or not. For those who won't admit it, isn't the love you have for your family real? Of course it is. But which of your five senses or what scientific instrument can you use to detect or measure it?

Unfortunately, as sinful human beings, we all know hatred is real. We've experienced both ends of it—wrongfully hating and wrongfully being hated. We all know through experience that loneliness is real. What? You thought you were the only one? I sincerely hope everyone reading this book knows through experience that love is real. So it's pretty obvious that the emotional realm is just as real as the physical realm.

The point is that we cannot understand someone else's emotions; in other words, we can't know the emotional reality of what they're going through unless we've experienced similar emotions ourselves. Just like in the physical realm, there are a plethora of examples to prove this point.

Help from a Friend

Why is it that when we're going through a problem in life someone who's been through it himself has more credibility talking about it than someone who hasn't? They could both say exactly the same thing and give exactly the same advice. If you think about it, the same advice is either just as good or just as bad no matter which person it came from. But we are much more likely to accept it from the person who's been through the same problem we're going through.

Why? Because they know what we're going through because they've experienced it! That, rightly, gives them more credibility and authority than someone who hasn't experienced it and hence doesn't really know what we're feeling or how hard it is.

Smoking

Having never smoked, I can still give all kinds of good advice and encouragement to friends who are trying to quit. I can tell them just what to do, and if they do what I tell them, they will be just fine. "I've read the most effective way to quit is cold turkey. So just don't light the cigarette." Easy, right? Not really!

I have no idea how hard it is, never having experienced it myself. Although I can give intellectual ascent to the power of addictions, only someone who has quit can understand, or know, what the would-be ex-smoker is going through, having experienced it himself.

The Baby Schism

Before I had kids, along with every other childless person in my office, I avoided new moms with baby pictures like the plague. What's the big deal? How can they sit for hours talking about the color of their baby's spit? Or worse! We childless but sane people got quite offended when new parents would say something smug like, "Just wait 'til you have kids. Then you'll understand." Like you have to have kids to know what it's like to have kids.

Guess what? They were right! There is a sense, a feeling, a mindset, a thing you get when you have kids that you did not have before. It cannot be described. It can only be experienced, and only those who have experienced it can understand it. You can't know what it's like to be a parent until you've actually been one.

Accepting the Unexplainable

Emotions are anything but rational. We don't expect them to necessarily make sense—they are emotions! We understand that there's a difference between the rational mind and the emotional heart and that we all have both.

Ever try to explain an emotion? Why did you fall in love

with your spouse? "Well, she had this quality that attracted me." Yeah, so do thousands of other people. Why were you attracted to that one particular person? Although we may understand a little of it, the truthful answer is, by and large, we don't know. We just were. It just happened. We can't explain it. But we all accept it as a reality of life.

Even the Bible accepts the inexplicability of love. Proverbs 3:18-19 (NAS) says, "I do not understand . . . the way of a man with a maid." And this was Solomon talking, the smartest guy in the world!

The point is, we don't throw out something just because we can't explain it. We pity those who don't allow themselves to love because they can't control it or understand it. And they're right—we can't control it or understand it. But, boy, are they missing out on a fantastic experience.

I hope I've convinced you by now that experience matters.

We might know *about something* (head knowledge), but we don't really *know something* (heart knowledge) until we've experienced it. Without our experience, we really have no clue about the reality of the thing in question.

So what's the point? We don't really know what we haven't experienced.

2

The Spiritual Realm

Izzy was having a bad day. It wasn't easy running a household in eighth century BC. He'd just walked a mile back to his tent in the cold, pouring rain, slipping often in the mud. He finally got back inside his tent, just in time to see his five-year-old son playing swords with a burning fire brand.

"What are you doing?" Izzy screamed at his son. When he heard his father yell, the boy started and dropped the fire brand right onto a pile of laundry.

"Are you trying to burn the whole tent down? How many times do I have to tell you? Don't play with fire in the tent! What do I always say? What's the worst thing that can happen in a tent?" he demanded of his son as he stamped the fire out.

"A fire," his son responded, in a very small voice. "I'm sorry, Daddy!" He started to cry.

"Yes, a fire! And what do you do? Start a fire! And why? So you could play! You burn down our whole tent, everything I've worked so hard for, but, hey, you had fun, so what the heck?" Izzy was way out of control, yelling at his son, and he knew it. But he didn't care. Ranting was how he dealt with stress, and this had been a very stressful morning. And besides, they were just words. So what?

His wife came in at that moment. "Oh, sweetheart, what's the matter?" she asked as she scooped up the boy and comforted him.

"Where were you? Our son almost burns the tent down and where were you?"

"Making your meal. Your favorite hot lentil soup is ready," she calmly answered Izzy. Then she said to their son, "It's alright now, honey. But you learned something today, huh?" The boy nodded vigorously. "Now go run along and play with something that's not burning, okay?" She laughed.

Her total acceptance and love of him made it all better. He hugged her neck and ran off to find something to play with that wasn't smoking.

"Look at this! Just look at this!" Izzy wailed, looking at the burned clothes. "Ruined!" he yelled.

"Had a tough morning?" she asked lovingly. "You look terrible."

"I had to fire Jonus this morning! And a darn cow bloated in the field last night! Dag-nab-it, do you have any idea how much wealth I've lost today? No, you wouldn't."

"Please don't be hurtful," she said, ignoring yet another insult. She saw something in this rough, brash man that no one else could. The Lord had shown her years ago that He was going to unlock her husband's heart. Early this morning He had told her today was the day. She was ready; she couldn't take much more of this.

"Why do I even talk to you?" was the kindest, more correctly, the least cruel thing he could find to say. He

The Spiritual Realm

hated himself for it. He complained at the air as he went off to eat his lentil soup. "Stupid woman. Stupid kid. Stupid cow. Stupid servants. Stupid rain." So what? They were just words.

He hated his wife for the same reason he loved her. Everything could be a mess, their whole life upside down, and she'd find something to laugh about. He hated it. It was really annoying when you were trying to have a bad day. And yet he loved her words. They warmed him inside. But he couldn't tell her.

Not for lack of trying, though. His words just came out dark and heavy and vile and . . . and . . . well, just unclean. But so what? They were just words. He'd told himself that enough times he almost believed it. Almost.

"Isaiah." Someone said his real name. And it was the most unusual voice he had ever heard. It sounded like a giant waterfall making words. He spun around and the tent was gone, or it wasn't; he didn't know, care, or even think about it. All he could do was focus, fixated, on what he saw in front of him. *I am undone* was his only thought.

In front of him he saw something language does not have words to describe. He saw the Lord, high and lifted up on a throne, with the train of his robe filling the temple. The Lord was blazing white with every color all at once, yet every color individually distinguishable and always changing.

When the colors shined on Isaiah, a different part of him sprang to life with each different pattern and shade and hue. The colors were living fabric, each one reflecting a different attribute of the character of God. The patterns and colors were never the same, they were constantly changing.

Yet the Lord Himself was totally constant—as if He

wasn't changing per se but just displaying a different part of Himself each moment.

There were angels flying about. Each time the colors changed, they would sing to each other, "Holy, Holy, Holy, is the Lord God Almighty! The whole earth is full of His glory!" They sang as if they'd just seen another attribute of God they'd never known about before, and all they could do was respond, "Holy, holy, holy." At the sound of their voices, the doorposts and thresholds shook, and the whole temple was filled with smoke.

Isaiah took in all this in a moment. Sound involuntarily came from his mouth. "Woe to me!" he cried aloud in terror. "I am undone! I am ruined! I am a man of unclean lips, and I live among a people of unclean lips, and my eyes have seen the King, the Lord Almighty!"

They weren't just words. They mattered. How could he possibly have thought any differently. Oh, no, how awful was the pain he'd caused by his words to the precious ones he loved. He saw himself for the first time.

Quick as lightening, one of the angels flew to the altar, grabbed a burning coal with tongs, flew over to Isaiah, and touched his mouth with it. He screamed and quickly touched the place where he was sure his lips had just burned off. Except his mouth was fine. In fact, it felt, well, free! As if, for the first time, he didn't have to say something ugly. He could choose, for the first time, to speak either death or life.

"See, this has touched your lips," the angel told him, holding up the burning coal with the tongs. "Your guilt is taken away and your sin atoned for." And then the most unusual thing happened. The angel smiled at Isaiah.

At that moment the Lord spoke from His throne. "Whom shall I send? Who will go for us?"

The Spiritual Realm

Before Isaiah knew what he was doing, before his head could catch up, he answered from his heart, "Here I am! Send me!"

The Lord smiled and nodded. "Very well then. Go to this people, and tell them . . ."

And the Lord gave Isaiah a message to speak to the people of Judah in His name. It was the first of many prophetic messages Isaiah would be given to speak for God.

The vision faded but not the change. He was back in his tent, eating his lentil soup that was still hot. How had he gotten to the table with the spoon in his hand? He looked very disoriented. His wife and son were looking at him strangely.

"Izzy? Are you all right?" his wife asked. "You zoned out for a moment there. You look like you've been to another planet."

"You have no idea," was all he could say, and then he started to cry,—something he had never done in front of them before. He felt pain, but not just because he was hurting or feeling guilty like always. This was different. He felt their pain—the pain he caused. And he was sorry for their sake, not for his.

He was sobbing now and couldn't stop. He expressed to his wife and his son things bottled up inside for decades that he wanted to say but couldn't before now. He told them about the vision and they believed him. Then he did something he hadn't done in way too long. He laughed. And they laughed together. And played. And sang. And lived. Something tangible changed in the tent that day and never changed back.

For years following, the Lord gave Isaiah some of the most powerful prophetic words he has ever given a prophet. They are still favorites today and bring healing to wounded people thousands of years later. And it all started with an experience. A spiritual experience.

—Based on Isaiah 6:1-13

Isaiah had an experience that changed his life when the Lord called him to be a prophet. It's so easy to read the Bible and gloss over what it must really have been like. It wasn't just some nice, neat, safe, esoteric spiritual thing. It was an unusual, very real spiritual experience.

Just like experience is critical to really knowing something in the physical or the emotional realms, it is just as important in the spiritual realm. We cannot know physical reality without experiencing it. We cannot know emotional reality without experiencing it. And we cannot know spiritual reality without experiencing it. We can learn all about it, but we can't really know it apart from our experience.

This is very hard for many Christians to accept. I will deal with the standard objections later, but for now, let's address the most important one we don't like to admit—having no experience with something means we're missing something. It's especially important when we've taken such pride in having gotten our doctrine right and see that experience can be messy and unpredictable. Often, we mature Christians don't do messy or unpredictable well, let alone both at the same time. Especially in church. We like to be in control. After all, whose church is it, anyway?

Ouch. Sorry. But I can say that because it perfectly describes my past. I didn't do messy. To quote Steve Martin in the movie *Parenthood,* "I don't like messy. It's so messy!"

The Spiritual Realm

And as an engineer, I certainly didn't do unpredictable. That is, until God crashed in and made an unpredictable mess of my nice, neat, comfortable, safe, little church life.

So I know this is going to be very difficult for some of us to accept, but it is nonetheless true. Just as it is true in the physical and emotional realms, so it is also true in the spiritual realm. We cannot really know what we have not experienced.

The point of Christianity is our relationship with God. What's relationship but knowing someone and experiencing his or her company? To actually know the God who made the universe and still loved us enough to die for us on a hideous cross even when we hated his guts is absolutely incredible.

Think back to the blind man trying to understand colors in chapter one. The colors are just as bright and real whether he can see them or not. But they are not real to him. They are only an esoteric concept with no relationship to his everyday life. Sadly, this is only too true with many of us and God.

Or consider the roller coaster example. Even though he knows all about the roller coaster, it's not really real to the PhD physicist until he actually rides it. Now in actuality, it was just as real before he rode it as afterwards. But it was not real to him until he rode it.

The same is true spiritually. God is just as real whether we experience Him or not. But experience makes God real to us. And God wants to be real to me. And to you. And this is where it gets dangerous.

If we let God actually show up for real in our churches, He may not stick to the liturgy. He might talk to us about our sin. He might show us our idols. He might even go for the throat and demand the one thing about which we've said,

"Anything but this, Lord." Actually, there's no "might" about it. Piece by piece He'll dismantle and destroy our little pretend games that we think have convinced everyone else we're okay. He'll come in and expect to take over. He's got this thing where He thinks he's God or something . . . maybe it's a Messiah complex.

People with Messiah complexes are nut cases because they really aren't the Messiah. But Jesus really is the Messiah; He really is our Savior. Unfortunately though, if Jesus actually went to a church, in some of them He'd be expected to sit down, shut up, and not rock the boat like everybody else. Read your Bible lately? Jesus perfected "rocking the boat" to an art form.

If God is allowed in the door, actually invited in, He'll want to open up places of pain in our lives that we've had hidden away for decades. Like a surgeon, He opens it up so He can heal that pain. The process of surgery, physical or emotional or spiritual, hurts and requires a recovery period. But then the area is healed.

But we don't want it healed; we just don't want it to hurt. We know good and well it's there, and we pretend it's not. We pretend we're okay, but we're really not okay, and we know it. But as long as no one else knows it, especially the people we impress at church, we're happy.

After all, we don't need healing. We've learned to cope. And coping keeps it from hurting, and that's what we want. Unfortunately, coping also keeps us from living.

Things that don't feel pain are not alive. What did Jesus say in John 10:10? "I have come that they might cope with all their pain, skillfully suppressing it so everyone at church will think they have it all together." No, somehow, that just wasn't it. What did He say? He said, "I have come so they may have life, and have it to the full."

But we cope; we don't live. Jesus wants us to live and live large. He sacrificed His life so we might have it. In order for us to have His life, He had to give it up. If He'd wanted us simply to cope, He could have just given up a group therapy session and skipped that whole cross thing all together. It would have been a lot less painful for everyone involved.

Experience Required

So God wants to be real to us. That means we have to experience Him. That's a spiritual thing, and most Christians are okay with that, even in church. They just don't want to get too emotional. Or do anything weird. Stay in control. Stay neat. They want to keep it Appropriate.

The word Appropriate is capitalized above because so often we have personified it and made it an idol, the true object of worship in our churches. We worship what we define as "Appropriateness" and will spiritually kill to defend it.

To physically kill someone means we remove them from our physical environment—permanently. Similarly, to spiritually kill someone means we remove them from our spiritual environment permanently; that is, they no longer go to our church. Now please don't confuse this with excommunication or accuse me of being against that biblical, hopefully rare, but sometimes necessary measure when someone won't turn from his or her sin any other way. That must be an act of compassion, an act of "tough love," to borrow Dr. Dobson's phrase. Excommunication is an action reluctantly taken resulting from unrepentant sin, but that's a subject for another book.

I hate to be the one to point this out, but offending our sense of appropriateness, or offending us, is not sin, and getting someone to leave our church because of it is nothing less than spiritual murder. We feel like they sinned and it produces such a strong negative reaction in us because what offended us is a sin against our false god of Appropriateness. But it is not a sin against the true God, especially when he's right there in the middle of it. Which God are we going to worship?

The Whole Enchilada

So why does it have to be so messy? Why can't people just sit quietly and experience God?

God is after the whole enchilada. He wants us to know Him and hence experience Him with our whole being—with our body, soul, and spirit. We're okay with the spiritual bit because we really don't understand it anyway, and so we can happily think it means whatever we are comfortable with. Then we feel good about ourselves and think we are cool. But making us look cool, of course, is not God's motivation.

But the soul is the mind, will, and emotions. While our mind and will may sit quietly and experience God, our emotions will not. Often, neither will our body. At some level all of our being, emotions and body included, must experience God.

Often the sheer power of the touch of God will make a person's body vibrate wildly. My former pastor once put it this way: "When the power of an infinite God touches a finite human being, that finite human being can't do anything but react in some way."

Okay, but why does it have to be so messy, so emotional?

When the God of the Bible, the God who created the whole universe, who split the Red Sea, who walked on water, who fed 5,000 people with only a handful of food, who healed with a touch and drove out demons with a word, who raised Jesus from the dead actually touches me or you, our entire being will react, one way or another.

Now please understand. Reading through the Gospels, or even through the whole of Scripture, it is readily apparent that God never does the same thing the same way twice. There is no magic formula. Sometimes God's touch is very quiet and peaceful, surrounded and protected by His presence and glory, building us up and revealing how deep and wide and long and high and thick is His love for us. But sometimes it includes battlefield emergency surgery, and it is anything but peaceful and quiet.

God wants us to be complete. Remember John 10:10? "I have come that they may have life, and have it to the FULL" (emphasis mine). Full, or some translations say abundantly, means complete. Every part of our being, spirit, body, and soul (mind, will, and emotions) is living life to its fullest, living large.

So it has to include our emotions because they are part of us, and God wants us to have a complete knowledge of him.

Going Where the Action Is

The other reason why it has to be so emotional is that often in our society, that's where the pain is. All of us have deep emotional wounds that need to be healed.

After all, God is the God of our emotions too. Or is He? A sure sign that we're worshipping the false god of Appropriateness is that God is not God of our emotions. We let God be the God of our minds—intellectual ascent costs us nothing, and it gives us that warm, snugly feeling. We'll let God even be the God of our wills—after all there are tremendous life benefits for living a godly lifestyle whether one knows God or not. And He can be the God of our spirits—we don't understand what that is anyway. If we're real Christians, real spiritual biggies, He'll even be the God of our bodies—"We don't smoke, drink, chew, or go with guys or girls who do." So we feel good about ourselves—what a witness!

But God of our emotions? Nope. That's too dangerous and can get too out of control. And it hurts. "He might bring up stuff I'm trying to forget and ignore!"

Might? There's no might about it—He will! He's going to go straight where the pain is if we let Him. "But I might cry and blubber and carry on and embarrass myself." Maybe. Maybe not. But if God is God of our emotions, we'll take that risk. I had a pastor who always used to say, "You spell faith R-I-S-K."

So the question should never be: "Is this really appropriate behavior in church?" Instead, the right question is: "Is this God?"

Necessary Experience

So experience, even emotional experience with God, is absolutely necessary. Note it is not necessary for salvation—emotional experience, or experience of any kind, is not necessary for that. All that's necessary for that is accepting Jesus into our lives as our personal Lord and Savior (Romans 10:9-13). Only God can judge another person's heart, so I'm not talking about salvation here.

But experience, even emotional experience, is necessary for knowing the fullness, the abundant life that God has for us. We could even say especially emotional experience because that's where our pain and wounding is.

It's a matter of degree—how much of God do we want in our lives? Are we only willing to turn over the comfortable areas where we look good? Or can He have all of us? Who really sits on the throne of our hearts?

I don't know about you, but I got saved at a relatively young age. But even so I didn't come out of the womb quoting John 3:16. We come out bawling; we come out in pain into a world of pain. I don't want to turn this book into a downer, but by the time I got saved, even as a kid, I was a damaged unit. I would not have made it past "quality assurance."

I needed, and still continually need, emotional healing. "Life is pain, and anyone who says otherwise is selling something," to quote the movie *The Princess Bride*.

So what's the point? Emotional experience with God is necessary to know the fullness of what God has for us because God wants our whole person, not just the safe parts we're willing to give Him.

We have to come to a place where we can let go of our sense of control and appropriateness and let God do . . . what? Whatever He pleases. If that means crying, then cry. If that means shaking and trembling, then shake and tremble. If that means intense emotions want to come out, then let them—don't hold them back. If it means sitting quietly and doing nothing visible while God deeply touches us on the inside while everyone else is crying and carrying-on, then that's okay too—we just close our eyes and focus on Jesus.

This should be a comfort to those who are nervous about this stuff: We are not trying to run a circus here or promote emotion for its own sake; we cover how to steward emotions rightly later in the book. But we are trying to be obedient to God. We are trying to create an environment where people are free to respond to however God is touching them, whether it's battlefield surgery or a gentle butterfly touch.

If we want to know the fullness of all God has for us, then we need to experience Him with our full being, including our emotions.

3

Common Objections

We cannot know what we haven't experienced, whether it's human love or an infinite God. In order to know God, we need to experience Him with our whole being, including our emotions.

Let's run through some common objections many Christians have to emotional experiences with God.

"Experience Can Be Unexplainable"

Translation: "If I as a pastor allow emotional experiences in my church, things may happen to people I don't understand and can't explain. How can I explain something I don't understand myself? What if they discover I don't have all the answers? They might find out I'm not the spiritual superstar I've convinced them all I am!"

Shorter translation: "Fear. I'm scared of what I don't understand." Fear should never be a criterion for what we allow in church and what we don't. "For God has not given us a spirit of fear, but of power" (2 Timothy 1:7 NKJV).

And I have a revelation for you, Pastor: The people in

your church already know you don't have all the answers, and they still come! They come because they're drawn to the vision God's given you for your church, and they feel God pulling, wooing, and calling them to be a part of it. They don't expect you to have all the answers; they expect you to lead them to God! Are you willing to do that?

Now we all know some of them do expect us to have all the answers. These people just want a nice, safe, warm, comfortable place where they can feel good about themselves but nothing actually ever happens. So if they didn't come to church for God in the first place, don't be surprised if they leave when He shows up.

Fear of people leaving is still fear and is not a legitimate motive for the man of God to decide what happens or doesn't happen with God's people. Don't worry, they might run from your church, but they can't run from God. And he will replace them and their finances with the people you really want, people who are running to God, not away from God. Wouldn't that be refreshing?

Now don't get me wrong. Everything that happens in a church is under the pastor's authority and covering. And to a degree he needs to understand what's happening so he can pastor what's going on. Note the choice of words—"pastor what's going on," not "control what's going on"!

But that doesn't mean we have to understand it perfectly, or at all, when it happens. We just have to properly discern whether it's God or not. And if it's God, regardless of all our fear, regardless of all the trouble we're going to get into from the people it offends, regardless of how much it offends me or you, let it happen. Pastor it.

Let people see you search out God to understand what's

happening. Let them hear you admit you don't have all the answers. Let them see the way you handle the unknown and where you go for answers and direction and wisdom. Let it be a good example for them. Then they can admit they don't know everything, are confused sometimes, often don't get it, and everyone can start being real. Sounds like a move of God to me!

"Experience Is Not Biblical"

I'm going to say something very controversial here that I hope won't be taken out of context, so I'm warning you up front. Please give me the courtesy of letting me explain what I mean before throwing the book out the window.

Experience does not have to be biblical to be God. To put in another way, it's okay if people's experiences are not biblical. Okay, there, I've said it. I realize this is a very explosive thing to say in some circles, so I appreciate your patience while I explain what I mean by it.

Let's define some terms here. What exactly does it mean to be "biblical"? In many Christian circles, something is biblical if there is an example of it in the Bible. For example, being a missionary is biblical because there are examples in the Bible (Paul, Barnabas, Silas, etc). Giving to the needy is biblical because there are numerous examples in the Bible and Jesus clearly lays out the principle in parables (e.g., the sheep and the goats, Matthew 25:31-46).

And it is precisely in this sense of the word biblical that I say experience does not have to be biblical. There does not have to be an example of it in Scripture for it to be okay, for it to be God.

This is quite easy to prove. The Bible itself testifies to its own incompleteness in John 20:31. This verse tells us why the Bible was written in the first place: "These are written so that you have an unabridged checklist for anything that ever happens to you or anyone else, so you can check the list and definitively know whether it's God or not, so you can set 'em straight without ever developing any discernment of your own."

No, not quite. What does it really say? "But these are written that you may believe that Jesus is the Christ, the Son of God, and that by believing you may have life in his name." Pay special attention to the previous verse, John 20:30: "Jesus did many other miraculous signs in the presence of his disciples, which are not recorded in this book." And then look at the very last verse in the book, John 21:25: "Jesus did many other things as well. If every one of them were written down, I suppose that even the whole world would not have room for the books that would be written."

See? God does many things that are not recorded in the Bible. Our infinite God will not be limited to the works recordable in any finite amount of pages, even His own. The Bible was not written to be an unabridged catalog of the works of God. Not every possible thing God can do was included in it. Far from it.

God will not be fenced in, even by His own book. That's not why the book was written. People who demand that everything that happens be duplicated in Scripture are in danger of worshipping the Bible instead of the Author. What a peculiar form of idolatry! The Pharisees made this mistake, you recall, and crucified the Lord of Glory. And Jesus had some choice words for them in Matthew 23.

I suggest another definition for the word *biblical*. I would say something is biblical if it does not contradict anything in the Bible. In this sense, experience very definitely has to be biblical. Nothing that happens to anyone should contradict the black and white words we do have in Scripture. If it contradicts Scripture, it is not God—there's no doubt about that.

However, experience can go awry at any one of these phases (which we'll go over more fully in the next chapter):

- Having the experience (revelation)
- Deciding what it means (interpretation)
- Deciding what to do about it (application/wisdom)
- Deciding when to do it (timing)

Just because someone misinterprets one phase doesn't mean the other phases weren't God. If someone has an experience and then goes and does something stupid (either blatantly violating Scripture or the common sense God gave us), that does not mean the original experience wasn't from God. Maybe he even interpreted it correctly, but botched up what to do about it due to a lack of wisdom in his life. And maybe God is using his mistake to teach him some wisdom!

"Experience Should Not Dictate Theology"

No, it should not. The Bible is the only source of infallible theology. But what does theology mean anyway? The prefix *theo-* refers to God, and the suffix *–logy* means "the study of." So theology literally means "the study of God." Yeah, right, like He's going to let that happen. At least not the test tube, scientific method kind we westerners are most comfortable with. God will not perform in our laboratory.

Now I'm not saying we shouldn't study the Bible. We

should. It's the Word of God, and it is the Light and life to all who read and follow it. And it leads us to God. But it's not God, and it should not be made an end in itself or the Word itself becomes an idol in our lives. We start worshipping the Word of God instead of worshipping God Himself.

And then at that point isn't this idolatry? Did you know the Bible itself can be an idol in our lives?

We can study the Scriptures all day and all night. We can learn all *about* God without actually knowing Him. The Pharisees and Sadducees who condemned Jesus are proof of this. They knew the Scriptures backwards and forwards, better than anyone, and yet they missed God, actually mistaking Him for Satan (Matthew 12:24).

Knowing the Bible does not make us spiritual; knowing God does. The Bible points us to God, and we should read it as much as we can. But reading it, memorizing it, and knowing it is not knowing or experiencing God. Reading it, memorizing it, and knowing it creates an environment in which we can know and experience God.

See the difference? The Bible is the on-ramp to the freeway, not the interstate itself. It's the glass that holds the water, not the water itself. If all we do is learn about God, study the Bible, even if we can fathom all mysteries and have all knowledge, we're no better than a crashing gong or a clanging cymbal to God (1 Corinthians 13:1-2). We think we are so spiritual but really we are just noise. The crux of Christianity is knowing God, not knowing the Bible.

"Experience Is Limited"

Yes, it is. Our knowledge of reality is limited to what we as limited human beings can experience of it. Our knowledge of God will never be complete. Did you expect otherwise? Experience is limited, but it's all we as humans have got to go on.

A German mathematician, Kurt Gödel, proved in 1931 some very interesting results, called the Gödel Incompleteness Theorems. Without going into a treatise of higher mathematics and logic, Gödel proved that even in the most logical of all the sciences, mathematics, there will always be theorems that cannot be proven. It's not just that we don't know whether they are true or false, just waiting for someone clever enough to prove them one way or the other, it's that we can't ever know everything. Gödel actually proved there are some things we can't prove. Ever. So God has built incompleteness, or limitation, into the very fabric of the universe. Nothing, not even mathematics, is complete in and of itself.

But even with its incompleteness, mathematics is still very useful. Without it, we would not have cars, computers, TV, radio, microwaves, iPhones, or virtually anything we citizens of the twenty-first century take for granted. We would never have gone to the moon or revolutionized the world without computers and the Internet.

So the incompleteness of mathematics is not a reason to throw it out. Would any parent really let his or her child say, "I don't have to do my math homework. Mathematics is incomplete so I'm not going to bother with it." I dare say this child is in for a rude awakening.

Likewise, our limitations are no reason to throw out experience. We don't throw out or avoid physical experiences because they are limited. No one would really say, "I don't listen to the radio because I can't hear the whole spectrum. I can't hear gamma rays or X-rays or ultrasonic frequencies so what's the point of listening to AM or FM?" Of course not! So why would we even consider throwing out or avoiding spiritual or emotional experiences with God because of our limitations?

"Experiences Are Diverse"

Yes, they are. No two experiences will be alike from person to person, just like no two people are alike. God made us all different, and it's okay. He's on top of it.

As limited human beings, it's easier for us to stay in control of things if all the things are the same. We reduce complexity by enforcing similarity. It's very effective. We stay in control this way.

But God is not so limited. To remain in control, God does not need to limit the number of different experiences possible. God is capable of touching each person differently at the same time and still remaining God in charge of it all.

Wanting everything to be the same for everyone is really intellectual arrogance. "One size fits all" is false any time human beings are involved. How can we possibly think we know the "everything" that should be the same for everyone?

Each person is in a different place and needs a different touch from God. And God gives each person what he or she needs at that moment, in that season of his or her life. God called us to be a functioning body, all with different needs and different roles and different strengths and different weaknesses, not a collection of irrelevant, identical, cookie-cutter earlobes. Is the message we really want to send the world, "Make Jesus your personal Lord and Savior so then you can lose all your individuality and become just like us"?

We serve a personal God, and He deals with each of us

personally. So we shouldn't expect our experiences to all be the same. Of course our experiences are diverse—they are tailor-made for each individual. And that's a good thing. It's a God thing.

"Experience Can Be Flawed"

Yes, it can. But none of us shuns physical experiences because they can be flawed. To do this would be to live in a rubber room: "I can't go outside today because I might perceive something wrong!" Unfortunately, we've made many of our churches spiritual rubber rooms.

But it's hard to argue with someone's experience. We really have no way of knowing for sure if he actually saw God or not, if he actually heard God or not, or if anything else he claims happened during his experience really happened or not.

What a mess this can make in a church, especially when everyone starts turning their experiences into theology to impose on everyone else! Many pastors shun emotional experiences for this reason.

There are numerous examples of abuse, bad teaching, and shoddy doctrine by Christian leaders who lead people into emotional experiences with God. We correctly identify the bad teaching and the shoddy doctrine, but then incorrectly discount everything else the person says or does and everything that happens to anyone who ever (past, present, or future) attends one of his meetings. We throw the baby out with the bath water.

Think about what that expression really means and what a tragedy it really is. If anyone literally "threw the baby out with the bath water," social services would have them jailed within the hour. Anytime we throw the spiritual baby out with the spiritual bath water, we harm the very people we are trying to protect.

The fear, of course, is that validating someone's experience can be misconstrued as validating all his doctrine—good or bad—or all the bad doctrine of wherever or whomever ran the meeting where he had his experience. So we make the opposite but equal error.

And this leads to our next objection.

"Experience Is Risky—It's Not Safe"

Now we're getting to it. This is the real issue. We Christians care deeply about people. And our leaders take their God-given responsibility seriously. They want to keep their people safe. And this is where it goes haywire.

In the popular children's book, *The Lion, the Witch and the Wardrobe* by C.S. Lewis, Mr. and Mrs. Beaver explain to the children about Aslan, the great lion they are about to meet, who represents Jesus and is going to save Narnia from the oppression of the White Witch. When Susan asks them if this great Lion, the King of the Beasts, is safe, Mrs. Beaver explains that most people who meet Aslan do so with their knees shaking. Mr. Beaver assures them that of course he isn't safe, but that he is good; he is the King.

What power would Aslan have against the White Witch if he was safe? What good would a tame lion do? Would she be defeated by watching him jump through a hoop? He's a huge, powerful, kingly lion. Of course he isn't safe. But don't worry—he's good.

Similarly, God is not safe. Coming into His presence will not be safe. If He were safe, He wouldn't have any power to set us free from our oppressions, addictions, and sins. But don't worry, He's good. He's the King. But in too many churches, we castrate people with safety.

Imagine the idiocy of buying a yacht and never sailing it. "I can't take it away from dock. It's not safe out there in the ocean. It might sink!" Yes, it might. Many have. But if we weren't going to sail it, which is what it was designed for, why did we buy it? We should have saved our money and spent it on something we would actually use, instead of wasting it on a boat we're never planning to sail.

The same goes for the church. We were designed to experience God. If God's touch is not going to be allowed in church, why are we wasting our time going? In our busy lives, half a day for church is quite an investment of an extremely precious commodity: time, especially on a weekend! If we're not going to do that for which we were designed, experiencing God, it would be more worthwhile to use our precious time doing something else.

But don't we want our church to be a safe place? A safe haven? Isn't the Lord a strong tower where we can run and be safe? (Proverbs 18:10, NKJV). Yes, but this is a different type of safety. This is safety from rejection, from oppression, from slaughter by the world, from the judgment we deserve. In this sense, yes, the church should be a safe place.

Letting people experience God's touch in church is risky and sometimes can go awry. People will make mistakes, the enemy will twist, turn, and pervert things (did we really think he would do nothing while people draw near to God?), and some things just won't make sense. But if it is God, it will be worth it—well worth it.

Experiences with God, even messy emotional ones,

should not be avoided because they are hard to explain, may be outside the box, or could be limited, diverse, or even flawed.

The adventure of experiencing God should not be avoided because of the danger of experiencing God.

4

Practical Discernment

I am Agabus of Judea. I am a Jew and a prophet of our Lord Jesus. I don't deserve to be—if you only knew what I used to be before the Lord made Himself known to me. But that's a story for another day—by the grace of God, I am what I am. And I have an urgent message to deliver. If I can only get there in time.

I'm on my way from my home just outside Jerusalem to Caesarea to see Paul. It's just over fifty miles as the crow flies but a bit more for me since I'm no crow. Getting over these dangerous mountains is what's taking the time—much more than I'd hoped.

I tell myself to just keep going. Not that the path is so physically dangerous, but bandits hang out in these lawless mountains. A lone traveler like me is an easy target.

The weather has been terrible and it's slow going. Maybe the Lord is using the downpour to protect me from the bandits. They'd need a pretty strong work ethic to attack me in this deluge, and fortunately that's not what bandits are known for. The road is littered with the remains of those who were not so fortunate.

A day and a half later and I'm out of the mountains

Mixed Emotions

alive. God is so good! And I am so wet. Wet, but alive. A good trade, I guess. All of my stock got soaked, but at least it's flat and relatively easy going the rest of the way to Caesarea in Northern Samaria.

My mind comes back to the urgency of my journey. Paul must not go to Jerusalem. The religious leaders there hold no love for Paul. He was one of them, you know, a Pharisee. He was their poster-child; his external righteousness was flawless. But then, when he least expected it, Paul met Jesus, and Paul has been preaching the faith he once persecuted ever since. So our religious leaders consider him a traitor and will falsely arrest him. The Holy Spirit has shown me this and sent me to Caesarea to give Paul this prophetic word. This is my urgent mission.

Finally I arrive at Caesarea, and there's the house of Philip the evangelist where the Spirit told me Paul was staying. But am I too late? No, there's one of Paul's traveling companions, Luke the doctor! Praise be to the Lamb, I made it in time.

"Luke!" I call out. "Do you remember me? Agabus of Judea."

"Brother Agabus, oh my word! Of course I remember you!" Luke drops his water bucket and runs to me, embracing me warmly.

"How long has it been?" I ask.

"Too long," he answers. The tears in his eyes at seeing me overwhelm me. I'd forgotten how much I love this precious and humble Gentile. Through his excitement he says, "The word you gave me from the Lord when I was last in Judea rocked my world. I'm still just beginning to unpack it. But what brings you to Caesarea? And alone? That's a long, dangerous journey."

Practical Discernment

"It is you who blesses me, Luke. Your faith and humility are an inspiration to us all," I reply. But now to the point. "I have a prophetic word for Paul. The Spirit has shown me you've been working your way down the coast by boat and will now turn inland and travel down to Jerusalem. But Paul is blindly walking into a trap. The Spirit has plainly told me he will be falsely arrested. He must not go to Jerusalem."

Luke's face falls. "If only. Maybe you can talk some sense into him."

"Luke, what are you talking about?" I ask.

The tears welling up in Luke's eyes now are no longer tears of joy. "We have indeed been making our way back down the coast. In every city the Spirit warns that prison and hardships are before him. Just last week in Miletus, Paul sent for the Ephesian elders. He told them this was the last time they would see him in this life. They begged him with many tears to not go back to Jerusalem, but he says he's compelled by the Spirit to go back, not knowing what will happen to him there. It's the same in every city where we stop."

My head is swimming. He knows? And he still heads for Jerusalem? "Luke, wait a minute, you said he doesn't know what will happen to him in Jerusalem?"

"Yes, that's right," replies Luke. "Not the details, only that prison and hardship await him."

"God be praised! That's the piece of the puzzle the Spirit gave to me and sent me here to warn him. Where is he?" I ask.

"He's inside with the brothers; come and see. I just came out to get us some water," Luke answers. "Come inside with me, everyone will be happy to see you."

And I am happy to see them. But none is happier to

see me than Paul. "Agabus, it does my heart good to see you! You can travel with me as far as your home in Judea. The Lord be praised to give me the kindness of your company!"

"Paul," I answer, "you must not go to Jerusalem or anywhere near Judea. The Jewish leaders there have been itching to get their hands on you for some time."

"Agabus, my friend. As a prophet, you of all people understand having to do what the Lord compels you in your heart to do. For the same reason you made that dangerous journey alone, I have to go."

Oh, the stubbornness of apostles! Does he still not get it? Okay, here we go. The Lord is giving me a picture for him. "Paul, give me your belt."

"What?"

"Just give me your belt. God wants me to show you something."

Paul mutters something about the stubbornness of prophets, takes off his belt, and hands it to me.

As the Lord showed me, I bind my own hands and feet with Paul's belt. Then I say, "The Holy Spirit says, 'In this way the Jews of Jerusalem will bind the owner of this belt and will hand him over to the Gentiles.'"

Now even Paul has to get it with this vivid picture. I can see on his face that he is no longer unaware of what is going to happen to him if he goes to Jerusalem. All the others who hear this begin to plead with Paul with tears to heed the word of the Lord not to return to Jerusalem.

Paul cries too, hugging the brothers, and then cries out, "Why are you all weeping and breaking my heart? This word of the Lord from Agabus has not come to prevent me from going to Jerusalem but so that I am prepared for what happens to me there. Luke, you

Practical Discernment

remember in Miletus I told the Ephesian elders I didn't know what would happen to me in Jerusalem? Well, now I know, thanks to Agabus, who has traveled a long and dangerous road to share this word with me. And this is an answer to prayer because I have been earnestly asking the Lord for the details. I am ready not only to be bound but also to die in Jerusalem for the name of the Lord Jesus. Thank you, Agabus, for bringing me this word, because now when it happens, I will be prepared and not dishonor my Lord with a wrong response as if something strange were happening to me."

What? Wait, no, what? The Lord is confirming in my heart what Paul is saying! But, I'm the one who got the word. Shouldn't I be the one to interpret it and apply it? But the Lord is telling me, no, not this time. In his body there are many parts, and while I got the initial word of the Lord and the interpretation, Paul correctly understood its application and the wisdom of how to use it.

What more can we do? We know in our hearts that Paul is right, but we don't like it because we fear for him. But we are forced to give up and acknowledge, "The Lord's will be done."

So we prepare to head inland with Paul for Jerusalem. I'll travel back with them as far as my home in Judea. It will be a much safer trip in a large group. We all make ready in our own way. There sits Luke, writing away, always writing. Who knows, maybe this will be worth a paragraph or two in one of his books.

—Based on Acts 20:13–21:15

We've made the point that we don't avoid emotional experiences with God because experience is inexplicable, limited, flawed, etc. It may be all those things and yet still be God. But I hear you asking that pesky question, "But sometimes it's not God. So how do we know whether it's God or not?"

I'm glad you asked. Answering that very important question is the subject of this chapter. In short, we learn and practice discernment. Sometimes it's difficult to tell whether the revelation is from God or just that thirty-six-inch anchovy pizza we had at 11:00 p.m. last night acting up. In this chapter, we'll discuss discernment in general, and then apply what we've learned specifically to emotional experiences with God.

While there's no magic formula, the process of discerning what is God and what is not generally happens in four phases. Discernment is a process, not an event.

The Four Phases of Discernment

Revelation. The first phase is revelation—having the initial experience.

So how do we get revelation from God? You don't. The fallacy is in asking the question; it reveals an unclear understanding of God. We can't get God to talk to us. We can't manipulate Him; He just isn't going to play any game we try to set up.

All we can do is place ourselves, as often as possible, in an environment where He is likely to talk to us, such as reading/studying our Bible, going to church, listening to good preaching, living every moment of every day like He actually cares about what we do, praying and worshipping at home. And then wait.

Simple, really. But it implicitly requires the inward core belief, or faith, that at some point He's actually going to talk to you. So while it's really rather simple, it depends totally on God.

But we as Americans don't like that. We'd much rather have it complicated and depend on us than simple and depend on God. So we come up with methods and jump through all sorts of convoluted hoops to attempt to manipulate God into doing what He wanted to do in the first place, if we'd have only given Him our faith instead of our methods.

Once having heard God, many people make the error of thinking that, while extremely cool, that's the whole deal. But this is only the beginning. There are still three more phases.

Interpretation. Interpretation answers the question, "What does it mean?" Without knowing the interpretation of a revelation, the revelation is useless.

Ezekiel got a pretty wild revelation from God that would have made the special effects team from the movie *The Mummy* proud. Remember the valley of dry bones vision in Ezekiel 37:1-10? God shows Ezekiel a valley filled with dry bones and asks him if these bones can live. Ezekiel, after many long years of service to God, has learned not to offer his opinion about what is possible and what is not. So he responds, "O Sovereign Lord, you alone know." God has Ezekiel speak to the bones, telling them that they will live, and they do! They miraculously come together and get covered by tendons, and flesh, and skin, layer by layer, until a vast, living army is standing before Ezekiel.

So what does it all mean? God Himself gives the interpretation in verses 11-14. Israel is currently in bondage in Babylon and thinks their nation is destroyed forever—they are like dry bones never to rise again. Against this backdrop, Ezekiel's vision is a powerful statement of hope for the Israelites. God is saying He will restore their nation, no matter how hopeless it looks to them. So you see that without interpretation, revelation is just cool special effects.

It's quite possible, and unfortunately very common, to get the revelation right and mess up the interpretation. This is like getting on the freeway at the right on-ramp but going the wrong direction. You just aren't going to get there.

Application/Wisdom. The application or wisdom phase answers the question, "What am I going to do about it?" The application is the wisdom of what to do with the information God has divinely provided. We can get the revelation and the interpretation right but mess up the application/wisdom and we're still heading in the wrong direction.

A good example is the story about the apostle Paul going to Jerusalem in Acts 21:10-15, dramatized at the beginning of this chapter. Paul is heading for Jerusalem, when Agabus comes to see him, takes Paul's belt, and binds his own hands with it. Then he says, "The Holy Spirit says, 'In this way the Jews of Jerusalem will bind the owner of this belt and will hand him over to the Gentiles'" (v. 11).

So that's the revelation. But what does it mean? Is it figurative or literal? Will Paul's ministry be hampered or bound, or will he actually be arrested? Based on previous revelations (Acts 20:23), they correctly decide it is a warning that Paul himself will be arrested.

So we have the interpretation, which wasn't too difficult in this case. What is the application/wisdom? What do we do with this? The general consensus is this means Paul should not go to Jerusalem (v. 12). This seems fairly obvious. So the brothers plead with Paul, even with tears (v. 13), not to go. But Paul has the correct application/wisdom in verses 13-15. He knows that while it is a warning from the Lord, it is not to prevent him from going to Jerusalem, but to prepare him for what will happen to him when he gets there.

Do you see the two possible but diametrically opposed applications? They agreed on the revelation and the interpretation, but over the application/wisdom they were worlds apart. And the correct application wasn't the obvious one.

Timing. People have a tendency to forget this phase even when they practice the other three. So we got it (revelation), we know what it means (interpretation), we know what to do about it (application/wisdom), but do we know *when* to do it? Maybe the revelation is right on, and we have the correct interpretation and application/wisdom, but it's for a year from now. Maybe it's for ten years from now.

David was anointed king at least fifteen years before he began his rule (1 Samuel 16; 2 Samuel 5:4). Joseph's dream about his brothers bowing down to him was given to him by God at least eighteen years before it happened (Genesis 37:2; 41:46; 41:53). Abraham and Sarah were promised a son twenty-five years before it happened (Genesis 12:2; 12:4; 21:5).

In correctly hearing God in our experience, it's equally important to get the timing right. Unfortunately, this is often ignored, and we say, "My pastor acknowledges the word I got is from God to the church and he says he knows the interpretation and the application/wisdom—so why isn't he doing anything about it?" Well, just relax—it may be a good word, but it may not be for right now.

The Big Error

The big error we tend to make is to throw out everything if an error is made at one phase. For example, just because someone botches the application/wisdom and ends up doing something really stupid does not mean the original experience and/or the interpretation were not correct.

This error works in the other direction also. Sometimes we think that because we got this awesome revelation, we automatically have a lock on the other phases. Nothing could be further from the truth. God often gives others the interpretation and application/wisdom (and the timing) because He made us all different parts of one body, each with different gifts, and it takes a plethora of gifts to make it through this four-phase process. There are no lone rangers in the kingdom of God.

Sanity Checks

Now let's discuss some general guidelines that should run throughout the whole process.

Consistency with Scripture. The Bible is still the yard stick to which all the phases are measured. Note that there does not have to be an explicit example in Scripture (see the discussion earlier of what's "biblical"), but nothing in any of the phases can contradict Scripture.

Practical Discernment

Wisdom in many counselors (Proverbs 15:22). Usually, if we feel we are right and the rest of the world is wrong, it's probably the other way around. Listen for trends. While not always true, in general if many unrelated people are independently telling us the same thing, we need to start paying attention. And don't just ask people whom you know are going to tell you what you want to hear. That's cheating. Ask people whom you believe have the greatest wisdom and discernment, especially if you don't always agree with them. If across an objective cross-section of independent individuals you're hearing essentially the same thing, then what they are saying needs to be seriously considered.

Ask your pastor. Pastors typically are filled with wisdom and can greatly aid in deciding what practical steps to take in attempting to walk out the revelation of God in our lives. They do not have all the answers, but they are experts in pointing us in the right direction.

Pray, pray, pray. Pray every minute of every day, in one form or another, as part of your lifestyle. Prayer is an essential ingredient, if not the essential ingredient, for discerning what is God and what is not. It's easier for God to talk to us, or more correctly, it's easier for us to hear Him, if we're already in a dialog with Him. God wants to give us revelation, interpretation, application/wisdom, and the timing. But we can't manipulate it out of Him.

Humility. Have honesty within your own heart. The Bible says God rewards those who earnestly seek Him (Hebrews 11:6). So if you are honestly seeking the truth, honestly looking for God, honestly trying to hear what He's trying to tell you, will not God reward your search by letting you find Him? Will He not give you the Spirit of wisdom and revelation (Ephesians 1:17)? Will He not fill you with the knowledge of His will through all spiritual wisdom and understanding (Colossians 1:9)? Of course He will. He will protect you and guard you, His face will shine upon you, and He will not let you miss His will for your life.

But if we are seeking revelation, interpretation, application/wisdom, and timing to satisfy our own needs and are living in rebellion to our church leaders then have no doubts we will go astray at the interpretation and/or the application/wisdom phases, until, if we do not repent, even our revelation will be corrupt and no longer from God.

Discerning Emotional Experiences

Discernment is a process, not an event. There are a couple of key questions we can ask to help facilitate successfully navigating this process.

Are people getting set free? This is the point, right? Are the people of God getting set free from their addictions and the strongholds in their lives? No one will know this better than your pastor so trust his answer.

Remember Jesus' answer to John the Baptist in Luke 7? John had done his bit to prepare the way for and testify to Jesus (Luke 7:29-30). Now John has been imprisoned for his troubles and is about to be beheaded. So if Jesus is going to bring the kingdom of God, John would appreciate it if he'd step on it. This is the backdrop to John sending messengers to Jesus asking (Luke 7:20), "Are you the one who was to come, or should we expect someone else?" Translation: "Hurry it up, Jesus, while my head is still connected to my shoulders!"

Practical Discernment

What was Jesus' answer in verse 22? "Go back and report to John what you have seen and heard: the blind receive sight, the lame walk, the lepers are cleansed, and the deaf hear, the dead are raised up, the poor have the gospel preached to them." The fruit of Jesus' tree—He was establishing the kingdom of God.

Objectively, what do we see and hear? Not what do we like and not like. Are people meeting God? If so, there should be a visible change in their lives. Maybe not that exact second, but certainly over time.

Are they wanting more from God? I was at a church where a lot of upper elementary and middle school kids were having emotional experiences with God. Is this God? Are they performing? Are they just wanting attention? They started showing up early for church—thirty minutes early!—and sitting quietly in the front row, just waiting for church to start. Thirty minutes is an eternity to kids. They just wanted more of God. They couldn't wait for church to start. Kids! You bet it was God.

In what direction are the people who are touched moving—toward God or away from God? A little logic here—Satan does not want us close to God. So if Satan is counterfeiting a move of God, the people getting touched are going to want to leave the church, not long to come into God's house to experience more of His presence. They may be all bubbly and excited for a short initial period, but it doesn't last and they quickly stop coming to church.

In a real move of God, the people touched have a lasting unquenchable desire for more of God. They want more of church, more worship, a longer sermon, and just plain more of God than they used to experience. They start reading their

Bibles; they start praying. They start living more of each day mindful of God.

Notice that I'm always talking above about the people who are being touched, not the ones who are not being touched, who are not having the emotional experiences that are causing so much controversy. If it's really God, those who did not come to church for God but came for some other reason will head for the hills. If those being touched are running to God and those not being touched are running away or even leaving the church (remember which direction Satan wants us going), then it's probably God.

Whose will do we want anyway? The following are not questions that will aid us in discerning the will of God, but, like the new disciples in John 12:43 ("they loved praise from men more than praise from God"), they are useful in discerning the will of people, if that's our desire. Whose will do we want done in our church?

- Does it offend someone, especially me? A sure sign we are worshiping the god of Appropriateness...
- Is it proper, appropriate, and/or polite? Ditto...
- Will it chase away the visitors? As if God needs our help to keep the people He wants to stay. Do we trust God or not?
- Do I like it? Unfortunately, if we are honest with ourselves, this is the most frequently asked and the most totally irrelevant question in trying to discern what's God and what's not.

Many of us don't ask these questions overtly. We are too smart (or sneaky or self-righteous) for that. A primer question, though, to see if we're really asking the above questions but not admitting it to ourselves, is: "Will this thing that's offending me keep these people from going to heaven?" If it won't keep them out of God's presence, why are we letting it keep them out of ours?

God will prayerfully lead us through four phases of understanding and walking out the experiences He gives us; namely, revelation, interpretation, application/wisdom, and timing. And God is such a God of grace—making an error, even a serious one, in any one of these phases does not invalidate the other phases.

5

Experience Leads

"He's your son! It runs in your side of family!" he shouted. It must be her fault.

"It does not!" she defended herself. Again. "Maybe it was your family. Maybe it was you!" She had never come out right and said it before, but she'd been thinking it. "All your drinking! All your drinking! That's the sin we're paying for!"

He raised his hand to slap her and then put it down. Tears welled up in his eyes. He was afraid of what he'd almost done, of what he was capable of doing. He turned away to hide his emotion from her. Must be a rock and not feel. His hatred of himself bumped up a notch. Again.

They were both at the end of their ropes. Sparring with each other was how they coped. They took out their frustrations on each other and then had an excuse to storm off and be alone. It made for a lousy marriage, but at least they didn't keep it all bottled up. But it was getting worse. After more than two decades of this, they each knew they couldn't take much more.

Thirty years ago, she was the most beautiful girl in all Jerusalem. The perfect Jewish girl, like Ruth, poor but noble, humble but honorable. He could do no better.

And she loved him, those thirty years ago. The perfect Jewish boy, like David or Moses, always wanting to do the right thing. He followed the law of Moses flawlessly from his heart like no other boy she knew.

Their marriage was a Jewish fairy tale, set against the tragic backdrop of first century Roman occupation. Two young people, deeply in love, committed to the Torah with their whole hearts. They were an inspiration to the whole community, even the rabbis said so. The first eight years of their marriage, while childless, had been heaven on earth.

And then it happened. The child they had waited so long for, now in his twenties, was cursed from birth—born blind. It had to be someone's fault. Everyone said so. What went wrong? Who sinned?

A temple guard burst in at that moment. "Are you the parents of that beggar everyone says was born blind?"

"Yes," they both stammered at once. What was a temple guard doing here? And what did he want with them? Hadn't they suffered enough? "Yes, our son was born blind."

"Then come with me. You've got some explaining to do." This was not a summons you could refuse. So they followed him to the temple, where all the Jewish leaders were assembled.

"These are the beggar's parents," the guard announced with contempt as they entered the courtyard. She hated that. The eternal contempt. *He may be the disgrace of our family, but he's still a man*, she thought.

Wait, was that a flash of anger in her husband's eyes as well? He hid it quickly and he hid it well; no one else knew, but she knew. And she smiled to herself. Maybe

Mixed Emotions

they still had something in common after all.

"Mom! Dad!" cried their son. He rushed to them instead of just holding out his hands and letting them come to him. It was almost as if he could see! What on earth was going on? They didn't understand, and that made them all the more afraid.

They were about to ask him when he embraced them. "I can see!" he cried. "I can see! Mom, you are as lovely as your voice. Dad, you look strong, just like you sound. Look, I can see!"

"What happened?" was all they could say.

"Jesus of Nazareth put mud on my eyes; I washed and now I see!" their son exclaimed again.

Okay, so that's certainly not a medically sterile procedure, but his eyes are different—they're normal! They weren't foggy or cloudy anymore—he really could see! Then this is a miracle, Glory to God! But then why does everyone but their son look so furiously angry? What is going on?

"You there!" boomed a very surly-looking priest. "Are you this man's parents? Is this your son?" He was very demanding. He'd obviously had a very difficult morning. And even with the prayer cloth over his head, you could tell he was also having a very bad hair day.

"Yes, this is our son," they said confusedly, still trying to figure out what was going on.

"The one you say—you say, mind you—was born blind?" the priest demanded, as if he didn't believe their son was really born blind. "Explain to us then how now he can see!"

Suddenly, they understood it all in a flash. Why everyone was so upset. Oh no. And our family's right in the middle of it. How do we get out of this?

Experience Leads

Jesus, that prophet from Nazareth who's been turning all Judea upside down, the one they tell all those exaggerated stories about—this Jesus apparently healed their son. A man born blind. Unheard of. Only one sent by God could do that. The prophets wrote that the Messiah would do such things. That makes this Jesus the Messiah.

But he can't be. The Jewish leaders had already decreed that anyone who said Jesus was the Messiah would be put out of the synagogue, the local Jewish "church" that every Jew went to. And he made mud with his hands—that counts as work on the Sabbath! God wouldn't break his own Sabbath, would he?

They were all looking at him. What was he going to say? If he said Jesus healed their son, he'd be accused of saying Jesus was the Messiah, whether he really said that or not. There would be no backtracking. They would be put out of the synagogue, ostracized, not even spoken to. No one would do business with them or sell to them. How would they live? This would be a hundred times worse disgrace on the family than everything they've suffered so far. And he knew he had about two seconds to prevent it, to protect what was left of his family.

"Yes, we know he is our son and we know he was born blind. But how he now can see, or who opened his eyes, believe me, we do not know. Ask him. He's of age; let him speak for himself." A dagger went through his heart when he said it, but he had no choice. The only way to save his wife and himself was to throw their son under the chariot.

Eventually they were dismissed—thrown out was a better description.

Outside, father and son argued heatedly. Like they always did. She hated it. How could the two people she

Mixed Emotions

loved most in all the world be constantly at each other's throats?

"But Dad—"

"Don't you 'but Dad' me! You can't even get healed without a controversy! You almost got us put out of the synagogue!"

She had had enough irrational argument for one day. "Stop it, both of you!"" she interrupted. "Your father saved our family the only way he could," she scolded their son. "And you," she said to her husband, "Look, honey, he can see! Doesn't that count for something?"

He looked at their son for really the first time. She had a point. "Okay, son, just tell us this. How could this Jesus do a Messiah-miracle in a way that broke the law of Moses?"

"Look, Dad," their son answered, "we know I was born blind, and we know this Jesus healed me, and we know how he healed me. Those are the facts. That makes him at least a prophet, if not the Messiah! But you're right, Dad. The Messiah wouldn't break the Law. So somehow he must not have. Look, I don't like it either, but what if he understands the Law better than we do?"

They looked at each other, all three of them. They all knew what that meant. If they couldn't even understand something as fundamental in Judaism as the Sabbath correctly, then everything was up for grabs.

The audacity of this prophet from Nazareth! The nerve of him to force this choice on them: whether to accept him and this uncomfortable experience and all the uncertainty of not knowing where it will lead, or to reject him and what they knew by experience to be true but stay in their cultural comfort zone, snug and safe.

Why did the true choice also have to be the dangerous one? Their dilemma was truth or safety. In the end, they decided. What decision will you make?

– Based on John 9:1-34

What do we do when our experience doesn't fit into our theology, such as in the story above? What if God shows up in our lives in a way that he either shouldn't or even can't? Or so we thought. Which comes first, our experience or our theology?

We would like to say our theology. We would like it if nothing ever happened that we weren't ready for—that we weren't theologically prepared for. We would like it if we could explain everything right off the bat, if everything made sense. Wouldn't it be nice, wouldn't it be safe, if God never did anything we didn't first understand? But God doesn't work that way. He isn't "nice," and he sure isn't safe. But don't worry, he's good.

If we're willing to let God have an active role in our lives, however, our experience will often lead our theology. It just will. Get used to it. God refuses to only do things we first understand. If he did, we would never grow. And frankly, God doesn't really care if what he does offends our theology, or even breaks it. In fact, often he packages what he does specifically to break it. Just to remind everybody involved who's God here—because we tend to forget.

God in a Box

The fictional (but plausible) story at the beginning of this chapter is based on the story of Jesus healing the man born blind in John 9, from the point of view of the man's parents.

Let's look deeper at the biblical account of this story, at what we know really happened.

The story in John 9 is an example of Jesus showing up in a way that's clearly God, but also in a way that God wasn't supposed to show up, according to the widely accepted, mainline, conservative, conventional wisdom of the day.

I'll summarize the story for you. Jesus encounters a man who is born blind. Jesus heals him so that he can see, but it's the way Jesus heals him that gets him into trouble. He could have just said "be healed" like in so many other healings he performs. But he doesn't.

Instead, he spits on the ground, makes the dirt into mud with his fingers, and sticks it on the guy's eyes. It's a good thing the guy was blind and couldn't see it coming—you could never get away with healing a deaf guy this way. Then Jesus tells him to go wash the mud off in a pool across town, which the guy does, and—SHAZAM—he can see! But Jesus is long gone and is nowhere to be found.

Eventually, the Pharisees investigate the healing, and they have to do some research before they actually believe the guy was born blind. They talk with his parents. But here's the problem: Jesus did this on the Sabbath when no work was allowed.

The Pharisees defined just the healing part as work, and Jesus had got on their bad side on several other occasions for healing just by speaking to the person on the Sabbath (John 5:8-16). But just to make sure he'd break (no, shatter!) their theology, Jesus had actually done work with his hands, making the mud.

He didn't need to make the mud; he could have just spoken and healed the guy as he did so many other times

(Matthew 9:1-8; Mark 2:10-12; John 5:1-15, to list just a few). But he made the mud on purpose, because he knew it would offend them. Anyone out there still think God is "nice"? Jesus wasn't just being an obstinate jerk, however. He was giving them a choice—the same one he gives us.

The Choice

Let's pick up the story with the Pharisees' investigation in verse 15:

> *Therefore, the Pharisees also asked him [the ex-blind guy] how he had received his sight. "He [Jesus] put mud on my eyes," the man replied, "and I washed, and now I see."*
>
> *Some of the Pharisees said, "This man is not from God, for he does not keep the Sabbath."*
>
> *But others asked, "How can a sinner do such miraculous signs?" So they were divided.*

Background. To understand their consternation and the choice Jesus was giving them we have to understand a little about first century Jewish culture. As we read the Old Testament, we see the following pattern repeated over and over again:

- Rebellion against God
- Defeat and oppression by an enemy
- Repentance and return to God
- Deliverance from the oppressive enemy

Mixed Emotions

Following the seventy year Babylonian captivity (Jeremiah 25:11; Daniel 9:2), they finally got it, sort of. They realized that being handed over to foreign oppressors was directly related to disobeying God. This was true, but they flipped over to the other extreme. A sect grew up in Israel, the Pharisees, which said we have to obey the law, so we're going to make sure everybody follows the rules. In fact, to make sure everyone understands the rules, we're going to write more rules, to clarify God's original rules. And over time, these extra written traditions came to have, in their minds, the same weight as the Scriptures given by God to Moses.

But these extra written traditions were all external, and Jesus is always concerned with the internal motivations of the heart. They missed the point that Moses' law was an example of the type of justice, devotion, and righteousness that would flow out of our lives if our hearts were right with God. They made the Law an end in itself. They worshipped the Law instead of the Law-Giver, much like some of our churches today worship the Bible and their associated doctrine instead of its Author.

To give you a feel for how corrupt, from God's point of view, how external, how devoid of any internal piety these rules really were, here's an example. Keeping the Sabbath meant "no work." They correctly discerned from the Scriptures that it is not a day to just do as you please and make money but a day that should be devoted to God (Exodus 31:15). Instead of teaching people to consider the motivations of their hearts ("Am I honestly doing this Sabbath day activity for God or for me?"), they externalized it. Big time.

In particular, it meant no business trips. So if you had an 8:00 a.m. business meeting Sunday morning in the next town, that was just too bad for you. You couldn't travel the day before, on the Sabbath. You had to deal with the morning commute. But wait a minute, I really want to travel the day before. So just how far can I walk on the Sabbath before it counts as work? It was decided that if you walked more than a mile (or the equivalent unit of measure in their day) from the border of your property, then it was work.

If the next town were two miles away, that was a problem. But wait a minute—not really. On your trip back Friday afternoon before the Sabbath, you dropped your coffee cup (or a cloak in their culture) at the one-mile point. As long as your coffee cup was within a mile of your property, it became technically an extension of the border of your property!

Then, for purposes of the Sabbath, you could walk to your coffee cup without technically leaving your property. And then you could walk one more mile to the next town. Sweet! If the town you wanted to go to was three miles away, you just dropped two coffee cups, each a mile apart.

Can you spell L-O-O-P-H-O-L-E? They had God so figured out, in such a nice, neat, little box, they even knew where the loopholes were.

You see how external, how devoid of any internal heart motivations, this had become, to the point of absurdity? This is the culture Jesus was trying to speak life into.

Back to the Choice

Jesus wanted to put them in a position where they couldn't accept both their external legalism and Jesus. He wanted to force a choice.

So he goes for the throat. Doing manual labor of any kind was expressly forbidden. That was work, everybody agreed on that, no controversy, no doubt about it. So Jesus made mud with his hands to intentionally do something he knew they would classify as work. And then he tells the blind guy to go and wash, which is also considered work.

On the one hand, we have a clear legal violation: breaking the Sabbath. God wouldn't break his own Sabbath, right? It's one of the Ten Commandments! So this Jesus guy can't be from God! But on the other hand, we have a bona fide miracle! He actually healed a guy born blind! How can we ignore that? And this is the stuff the prophets said the Messiah would do (Isaiah 29:18). So how could Jesus possibly heal a man born blind if he wasn't from God?

He couldn't. So he must be from God. But God wouldn't break the Sabbath, so he must not have really broken the Sabbath by doing this.

But then our understanding of what's breaking the Sabbath must be in error. But if we don't even understand how to keep the Sabbath (and we have spent hundreds of years figuring this out!), our whole understanding of the entire Law is up for grabs!

Well, we can't have that, can we? So he must not be from God, and we explain away or ignore the miracle.

You see the dilemma? Either Jesus is God and our understanding of Scripture is in error, or our understanding of Scripture is correct and Jesus is not from God, and we just ignore, disbelieve, or somehow write off that miracle. That's the choice.

They had God figured out. They had God in a box—defined by an acceptable set of parameters called "theology."

But Jesus came in a way that was obviously God—fulfilling prophesies about the Messiah—but intentionally outside their theological box.

That was the Choice. They could pick God, or they could pick their box. An unpredictable, dangerous, out-there, out-of-control, and uncomfortably infinite God—against their nice, safe, predefined, comfortable, but limited, theology. They picked their theology, their box.

Our Choice

So how about us? Which do we choose? God or the box we thought we had Him in?

True Christianity always challenges the idols of the day. The Pharisees had turned the law of Moses and the accompanying volumes of "clarifying" traditions into an end in itself—into an idol. So Jesus came in a very obvious way that appeared to them to violate the law of Moses as they understood it. They could pick their idol or they could pick Jesus (God).

In reality, Jesus never violated the law of Moses, or more properly, the law of God given to Moses. In fact, he fulfilled the law (Matthew 5:17). Jesus just violated the part that they added, the part that was important to them, their god of Appropriateness.

Similarly, today some of our churches have made the Bible into an idol, just like the Pharisees did. And, just like the Pharisees did, we often miss God because of it. So it shouldn't be surprising that God comes in a way that is obviously God (people are getting set free, wanting more of God, and getting closer to God) but this appears (to us) to be unbiblical.

But in reality, it is biblical; it doesn't contradict Scripture, just the interpretation of it that has become so important to us. God is challenging the idol in our safe little Christian life—our false god of Appropriateness.

Theological Changes

I had a friend I'll call "Robert," who wasn't too sure about all this stuff. Our pastor was encouraging these emotional experiences, and after a meeting where several of the church leaders had prayed for Robert, he told our pastor, "Well, you pulled out the big guns and nothing happened."

A week or so later in another meeting, I had the privilege of praying for Robert. Even before I started to pray for him, before I even got over to him, God fell on him hard and he started rolling on the floor, growling. This is known as "manifesting" and is sometimes what happens when the kingdom of God has a border dispute with the kingdom of Satan. Robert was experiencing a "kingdom clash" in his life. You can read about a similar event in Mark 9:20.

Our pastor happened to walk by and asked Robert, "What are you doing down there, Robert? I thought you didn't do this stuff?"

All Robert could say was, "Grrrrrrowlllll!"

I responded, "I think he's busy at the moment" and continued to pray for him.

Afterwards, after God had broken demonic strongholds in Robert's life, Robert went up to our pastor and said, "It looks like I'll have to change my theology." And Robert was okay with that!

How about you? My friend Robert chose God, letting God totally kick out the walls of his box because he was more committed to God's truth than he was to his own theology. Can we all honestly say that? Or have we got God all figured out?

Robert's experience led his theology, but since he knew it was God that was okay with him, and he let his theology catch up. We can only do this if we admit our theology, our understanding of God, is imperfect, and therefore needs to grow and change.

This can only happen if we're not emotionally (or intellectually or pridefully) attached to our theology. I'll say it again, there are the basic tenants of the Christian faith that are non-negotiable. Unfortunately, and maybe this says something about us, those usually aren't the ones we're emotionally attached to, are they?

It's okay for our experiences to lead our theology. And if we follow God into the uncharted waters where he wants to lead us, it generally will. But since it's God, it's okay. Don't worry, he will catch up our theology, but after we've accepted the experience that broke it. He's just like that!

6

Close Encounters

Bimbo. Floozy. Tramp. And worse. I've been called them all. Prostitute, when they want to be nice. But they don't normally want to be nice.

The truth is, I'm none of them. Or all of them. I don't know anymore. I just want to be loved. But I've been deceived by love. I trusted too easily. Men promise you the world, love you while you benefit them, and then throw you out like trash when they're bored with you and want something fresh. I hate them all. I use them now.

I was young and naïve with my first. Like a fool I trusted him and gave him my childhood. Here in Samaria we weren't as legalistic as the Jews of Jerusalem. After all, didn't I love him? What was the difference with marriage anyhow—it's the same as living together but without the fake ceremony to a distant God we barely believe in anyway. He said as long as we loved each other we were married in our hearts. And that's all that mattered.

Until my world was shattered when he went back to his wife and kids—which I didn't know he had until the day he left me. No wonder he didn't want to get married;

he already was! What was I supposed to do then? As a woman I couldn't work, and now I couldn't get married if I wanted to. Who would want me since I wasn't a virgin? What else could I do?

So I found another man, my second just like my first, who didn't care about being married. He would take care of me. He would love me.

He was the last man I ever believed. He left me for someone younger, thinner, prettier. He traded up, and I was out with the trash. Again.

What could I do in this culture? So I found number three, number four, and number five. But I was stronger now. Now I know what to expect. Love is not forever; nothing is. So I leave them before they can leave me. I trade up. I'm about to leave number six, and the fool doesn't even know it. He won't even see it coming.

No one knows how many. No one knows but me that I've had five husbands before the moron I currently live with. That's my secret, something that's my own.

It's not such a bad life. I just have to avoid the hypocrites; it's not worth bickering with them. The other women who are just afraid their husband will be number seven. And they should be. They just wish they could trade up, but they're married—they're stuck.

So I come out here to the well in the heat of the day. No one else is ever out here now. Oh no, who's sitting on the well? A Jew, and a Rabbi no less, telling from his clothes. Great. A hated Jew. Those Jews in Judea think they're all that. They think they're the "real Jews," and they call us Samaritans half-breeds. They hate us, and we hate them for hating us.

So what's he doing out here anyway, alone, all by himself, in the heat of the day, so far from Jerusalem?

Mixed Emotions

Who cares? At least he won't talk to me, and we can just ignore each other. Jews don't talk to Samaritans, and men in both cultures don't talk to women. This is safe and boring. I'll just ignore him, get my water and go, and he'll certainly ignore me.

"Will you give me a drink?" he asks me. Startled, I drop my bucket and almost fall in the well catching it! What did he say? Is there someone else here?

"Excuse me, sir, what?" I stammer to buy time. He did not just talk to me.

"Will you give me a drink, please?" he asks again. Kindly. Matter-of-factly. As if a Jewish man talking to a woman, much less a Samaritan, is no big deal! I have no value in the world, and he's all that. Doesn't he know the rules?

"You are a Jew," I sneer, "and I am a Samaritan woman." Emphasis on the last word, in case he didn't notice. "How can you ask me for drink?"

"If you knew the gift of God and who is asking you for drink, you would have asked him, and he would have given you living water," he answers.

One of us has been out in the sun too long. "Sir," I answer and laugh, "the well is deep and you have no bucket. Where will you get this living water?" Whatever that is. "Are you greater than our father Jacob who gave us this well? He drank from it himself, with his sons and all his flocks and herds." Who does this guy think he is?

"Everyone who drinks this water will be thirsty again," he babbles on. "But whoever drinks the water I will give him will never thirst. In fact, the water I give him will become a spring of water welling up inside him to eternal life." What? Never get thirsty again?

Okay, I'll bite. I'll call his bluff. "Sir, give me this living water so I won't get thirsty and have to keep coming here to get water." That ought to end this conversation quickly.

He answers, "Go call your husband and come back."

Oh no, we are not going there! "I have no husband," I say truthfully. There's one advantage to not being married.

"You are right when you say you have no husband," he says. "The fact is, you have had five husbands, and the man you're living with now is not your husband. What you have just said is quite true."

How does he know that? No one knows that! He can't know that! No one knows how many but me. And he said it so kindly, complimenting me for telling the truth when he knows I just lied to him! But if he knows, why is he still talking to me?

"Sir, I can see that you are a prophet," I say as confidently as I can, to hide that I'm reeling inside, but I'm sure he heard my voice crack. This is getting way too personal; time to change the subject. "Our fathers have worshipped on this mountain for generations. But you Jews claim the only place to worship is in Jerusalem." There. A good theological controversy. Back to safer ground where we hate each other. Now he can tell me how wrong we Samaritans are, and I can insult him back, get my water, and go.

But instead he says, "Believe me, woman, a time is coming you will worship the Father neither on this mountain nor in Jerusalem." What did he just call me? Woman? Not a name? Just woman? That's the most respectful way he could have addressed me in this culture! Why is he talking to me like this, like . . . like I have value?

"You Samaritans worship what you do not know, but

Mixed Emotions

we worship what we know, for salvation is from the Jews," he continues. He just says it like facts, no condemnation in his voice at all. And why do his eyes stir my heart so? "Yet a time is coming and has now come when true worshippers will worship the Father in spirit and truth, for those are the kind of worshippers the Father seeks. God is spirit, and those who worship him must worship in spirit and in truth."

He talks as if he knows this stuff first hand but without being arrogant about it. This is too much for me. Gotta get out of this conversation, so I just say, "Well, I know the Messiah is coming. He'll explain everything to us." My head is screaming to get my water and get out of here, but what is in those eyes?

Then he says to me, "I who talk with you am he." The Messiah? In my heart I instantly know it's true. Don't ask me how I know, but I know.

Acceptance! That is what I see in his eyes! Affirming me, giving me value. I didn't recognize it; I've never seen it before, not even from my parents. I have no value or my own parents wouldn't have rejected me.

But there's this love in his eyes I can't turn away from. A love like I've never known before, freely offering me friendship and conversation and acceptance with no strings attached, no manipulation. As if I was more important than my sinful life. He honors me and values me and treats me like a... a person. I've never experienced this before! Can my whole life change in a moment? Well, I think it just did.

I fall at his feet and sob. He gently picks me up, sits me on the well, and draws my water for me. "Marta, go call Ibrahim." He knows my name. And Ibrahim, my not-husband. He knows his name, too. Of course he does;

he's the Messiah. Something's welling up in me. What is this? Is this what it's like to experience love? Real love, true love, with no deception or hidden agenda. I know somehow that meeting this man has changed my world and my heart forever in ways I don't yet understand. I forget the water and run back toward the town. Yes, I'll get Ibrahim. I'll get the whole town...
– *Based on John 4:1-29*

In this chapter, I want to go through several other examples of people who were changed forever, not because they finally got it right intellectually or theologically, but because they experienced God.

The Woman at the Well

This story is recorded in John 4:1-42. I dramatized it at the beginning of this chapter, from the woman's point of view, and hopefully put some skin on it. Let's dive into it a little deeper.

While his disciples are in town getting takeout, Jesus strikes up a conversation with a Samaritan woman. This is remarkable in a couple of ways.

About three hundred years previous, the Assyrians conquered Samaria, the northern kingdom of Israel. In those days, you didn't just exile the people you conquered, you exiled half of them to a second conquered country, bringing half of the second conquered people to the first conquered country. So you mixed up and diluted their ethnicity; it made them easier to control since there wasn't a sense of national or ethnic pride. So the Jews in Judea thought they were the "real" Jews, and the Samaritans were just half-breeds. The Jewish/Samaritan hatred ran so deep that many Jews would spend extra travel days going completely around Samaria, and the Samaritans wouldn't even sell to you if you were going to Jerusalem.

So Jesus' initiating a conversation with a Samaritan was very radical in that culture. (See verse 9: "For Jews do not associate with Samaritans.")

The other thing that made this quite progressive was that Jesus talked to a woman, again very unusual in that culture (v. 27). In fact, this might be the first recorded instance of women being treated like human beings in the Middle-Eastern world. The male Jews of the day had a prayer they would say: "God, thank you that I am not a Gentile or a woman."

Women were treated as property, as chattel. Unfortunately, they still are in most Middle Eastern countries, except Israel and a few others. In many Arab countries today, women have to walk ten feet behind their man.

Jesus breaks multiple cultural taboos by striking up a conversation with this woman, asking her for a drink. They chat for a bit. Jesus finally reveals the sin in her life but in an absolutely noncondemning way (vv. 17-18), when he speaks to her of her sexual sin. Her secret sin that only she knows. Her current lover probably knew he wasn't the first but probably didn't know how many preceded him. Nobody but she knew that.

Nobody but she and this intrusive Jewish guy who according to the custom of the day should despise her for being a Samaritan and belittle her for being a woman, but who is actually talking to her like a human being. Others know her sin, and they either condemn her for it or participate in it with her—both driving her further from God.

But this Jesus guy knows she could be stoned under the law of Moses (Deuteronomy 22:20-27) and yet accepts her. In fact, it's obvious to her now that he knew her sin when he originally asked her for a drink. God, up close and personal.

Experience with God often boils down to that—God revealing who he is in our personal place of pain and brokenness in a way that's real to us. Conservative Christians tend to condemn the person while liberal Christians tend to condone the sin—while Satan's thrilled with either error since both drive sinners away from God instead of to him. We both have it exactly backwards while patting ourselves on the back for not making the other's mistake! But Jesus revealed the truth about her sin and himself while demonstrating his love for her by treating her as a human being, all without either condoning her sin or condemning her.

The experience, not the theological discussion about where to worship, changed her life. This woman, who would intentionally wait for the heat of the day before schlepping heavy water jugs to avoid social contact, went into town and told everyone she could find about "a man who told me everything I ever did" (v. 29). The change in her was radical enough for many to believe right there (v. 39). They came in droves to see him, and that experience changed their lives as well (vv. 40-42).

Don't you think she knew sleeping around was wrong? Of course she did—that's why she was out there in the heat of the day. But that esoteric, theological knowledge didn't make a difference in her life. Experience with Jesus did!

And it wasn't the theological insights Jesus gave her that

changed her life either. She didn't say in verse 29, "Come, see a man who taught me this neat theology about living water." She didn't say, "Come, see a man who finally resolved that pesky controversy over where to worship." No. It was what he did for her—"Come, see a man who told me everything I ever did." Her personal experience with God, not her theology, is what was effective both in changing her life and in evangelizing others.

Matthew and Zacchaeus

First, a bit of background. Matthew (or Levi) and Zacchaeus were tax collectors, Jews who worked for the Romans. Their fellow Jews considered them traitors. To put it in perspective, consider how the French felt about their countrymen who assisted the Nazis during the German occupation of France in World War II. Or what if the Soviet Union, instead of disintegrating during the 1980s, had actually taken over America? How would we feel about Americans who profited by helping the Soviets by doing their dirty work for them? We would treat them like the scum of the earth. They would be more hated then the occupying Soviets themselves. The Soviets would be at least oppressing an enemy—but these people would be betraying their own country, their own family, their own friends and neighbors.

The first century Jewish tax collectors profited big time from their association with the Romans at the expense of their own people. It worked like this: A contingent of Roman soldiers accompanied the tax collector from house to house. You had to pay up right then and there. Except the amount was variable, whatever the tax collector wanted at the moment. The tax collector set his own salary by collecting any amount greater than the amount he was required to collect by Rome. The amount required by the Roman officials was sent to them, and the tax collector pocketed the difference as his salary.

If you couldn't pay when he visited you, he could take anything he decided he wanted from your house, and the accompanying Roman soldiers would enforce his decision. If he saw something he wanted in your house, perhaps a family heirloom or anything of value or quality, he could arbitrarily raise your tax to a level he knew you couldn't pay so he could confiscate (steal) whatever it was he wanted in your house.

And there was absolutely nothing you could do about it. If you resisted, the soldiers would kill you on the spot. It was no wonder the Jewish people hated the tax collectors; we would too.

But Jesus not only was friendly and civil to them, he ate at their house—the token of friendship and acceptance in their culture! This got people's noses out of joint almost as much as his healing on the Sabbath. In our American conservative Republican Christian culture, this would be equivalent to eating and hanging out with the homosexual crowd, or with abortion doctors, or executives in Planned Parenthood.

Following Jesus, knowing what's God and what He wants for us, is really not that difficult when you stop to think about it. It's reconciling that with our own personal prejudices and desires, trying to find the "loopholes," that gets complicated.

But both Matthew (Matthew 9:1-13) and Zacchaeus (Luke 19:1-10) had their lives changed forever by this rude dinner guest who invited himself and his twelve friends over for dinner. Matthew became one of those twelve friends, one of Jesus' twelve disciples, completely giving up his profession and later martyred for Jesus, as were the other disciples. Zacchaeus, that very night, gave half of his possessions to the poor and committed to paying back everyone he stole from 400 percent (talk about interest!).

Jesus knew Zacchaeus' repentance was genuine because in Luke 19:9-10, he says, "Today salvation has come to this house, because this man, too, is a son of Abraham. For the Son of Man came to seek and to save what was lost."

Jesus did not pull off these amazing life transformations by having an intellectual debate with them. It was experiencing his presence, finally meeting him and knowing him, that changed their lives forever. They couldn't go back. They were different people now.

Moses, Isaiah, and Jeremiah

Each of these mighty men of God had powerful personal experiences with God first, before they had powerful ministries. Moses had the burning bush in Exodus 3 and 4, Isaiah actually saw the Lord in Isaiah 6, and Jeremiah was personally called by God in Jeremiah 1. They all went on to impact the world powerfully because they knew God through personal experience, not just about Him.

In all of these experiences, God never once addressed their theology. He dealt with things that were real to them, that would interfere, at least in their minds, with their service to Him. He dealt with Jeremiah's feelings of inadequacy (Jeremiah 1:6-7) and fear (Jeremiah 1:17-19). He dealt with Isaiah's verbal sin (Isaiah 6:5-7). And He dealt with Moses' long list of excuses (from insecurity to stuttering) in Exodus 3:11–4:17.

And it was out of their relationship with God, their experience of Him, that they endured being thrown down a well (Jeremiah 38:6), being sawed in half (Hebrews 11:37, presumably Isaiah—not in Scripture but Jewish tradition), almost stoned (Moses—Exodus 17:4), and numerous other trials they endured for serving God.

Paul

Talk about a guy who had it together theologically! In Philippians 3:5-6, Paul described what he was like before meeting Jesus: "Circumcised on the eighth day, of the people of Israel, of the tribe of Benjamin, a Hebrew of Hebrews; in regard to the law, a Pharisee; as for zeal, persecuting the church; as for legalistic righteousness, faultless." But he didn't know God—he had never experienced the Lord of glory.

He missed God so badly that he helped those who murdered Stephen (Acts 7:58; 8:1—he was called Saul at that time). He himself launched a great persecution against the church (Acts 8:3).

Why? Because he didn't know the Scriptures? No, he was a Pharisee and an expert in the Scriptures. But while he knew about God, he didn't know (experience) God. Without experiencing (knowing) God, all his theology was worthless. Paul himself says that as he continues in Philippians 3:7: "But whatever was to my profit I now consider loss for the sake of Christ. What is more, I consider everything a loss compared to the surpassing greatness of…" Of what? Of having proper theology? Of understanding the solution to the circumcision controversy that was going around back then, about which Paul was very passionate? Of reading the Scriptures? No. He says in verse 8: "Of the surpassing greatness of knowing Christ Jesus my Lord, for whose sake I have lost all things."

Paul had a tremendous experience with Jesus while on his way to destroy the church in Damascus, as recorded in Acts 9. This changed his life. Afterward, he spent considerable time in Antioch getting his theology straight. But he rarely references this time. Instead, he talks about his experience with Jesus on the Damascus road. Even after being saved, no one had better theology than Paul. He wrote the majority of the New Testament from which we derive our theology. He even corrected Peter (Galatians 2:11-21)! But it was his direct, firsthand knowledge of God, not about God, his experience of his relationship with God, that drove him to turn the world upside down.

Marriage

It's the same as marriage—the point is not knowing about your spouse, but knowing your spouse through experience with that person. Don't you know couples who are dealing with divorce because of a husband who's a workaholic and never spends any time with his wife? She knows all about him: his title in his company, how much his portfolio is worth, what degrees and honors he earned in school. But if they don't experience each other by spending time together, the marriage is in serious trouble. What's the common thing the wife says? "I just don't feel like I know him anymore."

Think about that. She doesn't know him because they don't experience time with each other. So the relationship goes down the tubes. After all, what is relationship but experience? It's experiencing time with the other person. In the same way, we can't claim we know God if we aren't experiencing Him. And true experience is messy, especially when God is involved.

God will change your life through your experience with Him, not through your theology, if you let Him.

I'm not saying we shouldn't pursue sound theology; we should. I'm just saying we shouldn't worship it or become emotionally attached to it. Because He will break it as He reveals more to us about Himself.

7

Incomplete Experience

Simpletons and fools. People are so naive. Like cattle. Fortunately. It's a good business if you're clever enough, like me, to capitalize on it. Do a few illusions and the gullible masses will follow you anywhere. And more importantly, pay you anything. Heal someone you plant in the crowd, split the profits with him later, and you've got yourself a real cash cow. Ka-ching!

This is my territory—First Century Samaria. I am Simon the Sorcerer. Let's see, what huge crowd have I drawn today? I round the corner and...

Where is everyone? There's no one here but Snubs and Wink, my less-than-average associates. If they've done something to mess this up...

"Uh, no one's here, boss," Snubs informs me. Thank you, Captain Obvious!

"Yeah, uh, nobody. Exceptin' us, of course. We're here," says Wink.

Getting something out of these two was like getting a commitment from a politician. You could do it but you really had to work at it, and even then it might not be what you wanted.

Incomplete Experience

"I can see that, you idiots!" I snap at them. "Where is everyone?!?" I slam my fist down on a brick half-wall for dramatic effect. But my wrist hits the corner of the brick way too hard.

"Aarrrgggg!" I howl in pain. I just broke my wrist!

"Boss! What happened?" asks Wink as he grabs my wrist.

"Aarrrgggg!" I howl again!

"Feels like a broken wrist. What's your diagnosis, Dr Snubs?" asks Wink before I can kill him.

Snubs suddenly grabs my broken wrist. "Aarrrgggg!" I howl yet again!

"Yep, I concur, Dr Wink. That's a broken wrist alright," says Snubs to Wink. He then informs me, "Ya got a broken wrist there, boss. Does it hurt?"

I will turn them both into a newt!

"We could take him to see that Philip guy, Snubs," says Wink. "He could heal it."

"What Philip guy?" I demand. More painful than my broken wrist is them knowing something I don't. There is no cosmic justice in the universe.

"The guy doing all the miracles down by the river," says Snubs. "It might take a while to get through the whole crowd that's usually here to see you, though, boss."

"What?" I snarl. "Somebody's moving in on my turf? And taking my public?"

"Yeah," says Wink, "that's why nobody's here. They're all down by the river watching Philip do miracles, talking about some dead guy who's not dead anymore, and then they all go swimming. We were trying to tell you when you walked up and changed the subject, breakin' your wrist and all. You shouldn't do that, boss."

Mixed Emotions

"Take me to see this Philip guy!" I command. I cradle my broken wrist as we march off, but I can hardly feel the pain over my anger. Nobody moves in on my turf. We'll see about this!

We finally make it to the river. There! That must be that Philip guy that everyone is staring at. I shove my way through the crowd. *My* crowd, by the way, that should be watching me!

I assess him quickly. He's wearing a simple robe, no astrological symbols even—c'mon, dude, you have to at least look the part—no sense of presentation. And he's just talking in a normal voice to people—no dramatic flare—no showmanship. What a loser!

He's probably healing someone he planted in the crowd. "In Jesus' name, be healed," he says. Jesus? The dead guy from Nazareth? I almost split a gut laughing. You do fake healings in your own name, so everyone thinks you're the big man. Didn't this guy take Fraud 101? What a bozo!

I've finally gotten right next to him when he speaks to me first: "Simon. Your name is Simon."

"Well at least you researched the competition, genius. Listen, pal, you're so terrible I'm gonna keep this simple," I say to him. "This is my turf, so just shove off, alright?" He looks at me like I've got antlers. "Hey, pal," I continue, "Don't play dumb with me or I'll ..."

"Your wrist is broken," he interrupts my threat, which is just rude. "Would you like it healed?"

"How much?" I ask. Might as well scope out the competition's prices.

"Free," Philip laughs. "Freely we received, freely we give."

"Okay, pal, now that's just not cool, undercutting

Incomplete Experience

prices to drive the competition out of business," I scold. "That's an anti-competitive practice, buddy, and you're gonna answer to—" He interrupts my threat again by lightly touching my broken wrist.

"Be healed, in Jesus' name" is all he quietly says. There's a loud bone pop that stings like fire for an instant, and then I can move it, pain free! It's completely healed! How'd he do that?

I stare at him, eyes wild. Now he's touching a crippled boy. Wait, I know that kid. He's been lame from birth. Philip says, "Walk in Jesus' name," helps him up, and he's walking! What is happening here?

Philip's no charlatan like me. People from the town that I know are getting healed all around me. And even if I didn't believe that, I can't doubt my own healed wrist. And he wants nothing for it? He could make a fortune with talent like that!

He's telling us about whom? Wait, Jesus, the dead guy, and He came back to life? But what if it's true? The question nags at me. The real miracles, not fakes like I do, speak for themselves. Something is coming alive in my heart. I believe! Time to go swimming!

"I believe! Philip, baptize me!" I cry out, and Philip does. I go down into the water a sinful, wretched, lying conman, and come up a new creature in Christ Jesus! This is the most phenomenal thing I have ever experienced!

Weeks pass. I follow Philip everywhere, fascinated by real miracles of God. Then one day he's gone. He's standing right there, there's a sound like a huge wind, and he's just gone. Weird.

We continue to meet in houses to talk about Jesus and fellowship together. But we really don't know anything; in fact, we're all pretty clueless.

Mixed Emotions

It has meant a change of lifestyle for me. Not for the better, mind you, but I'm happier with Jesus in my heart and not angry at the world anymore. But it's a harder life, and I'm getting really bored. Since Philip left, there's been no fireworks, no miracles. Ordinary life is so ordinary. But I'm not bitter or anything. I have a joy inside me now, but still . . .

Then one day Peter and John come from Jerusalem. They teach us about the Holy Spirit. We had just been baptized into Jesus by Philip; we didn't know anything about the Holy Spirit.

Peter and John lay their hands on people and pray for them to receive the Holy Spirit. People spontaneously burst out in other languages, faint, cry, laugh. This is wild! And all by the laying on of Peter's and John's hands. But they're going back to Jerusalem soon, and how will the people of Samaria get the Holy Spirit then? Hey, clever man that I am, there's an idea brewing. Maybe there's a way to get my old lifestyle back. Ka-ching!

I work my way over to Peter and John and get them alone. "Peter, John, listen. I've got a great business proposition for you. It'll fund your benevolence work in Jerusalem and keep the Holy Spirit revival experience going strong here in Samaria indefinitely. I have a huge store of money from the old days, if you know what I mean," I say with a wink. I told them how much and their eyebrows raised, and they looked at each other. I think we're going to have a deal here! "I'll pay you this money and you give me the ability to impart the Holy Spirit!"

They just stare at me.

"I know, right?" I continue. "I'll send you a percentage every month. Everybody wins." Finally, I'm able to use my good business sense for the kingdom.

Incomplete Experience

Peter speaks, but it's not the kudos I expect. "May your money perish with you, Simon," Peter says sternly, "because you thought you could buy the gift of God with money! You have no part of this ministry because your heart is not right before God!"

"Repent of this wickedness, Simon," John adds earnestly, "and pray to the Lord. Maybe He'll forgive you for having such a thought in your heart. We can see that you're still full of bitterness and captive to sin."

All I can do is stammer, "Hey, sorry guys, rewind. Pray to the Lord for me so nothing you've said happens to me!" They do pray for me, and I pass out under the power of the Holy Spirit. I've never felt such a change in my heart before.

But now they've gone back to Jerusalem. Where will our next experience come from? Hey, clever man that I am, I have another idea brewing. Jesus had twelve apostles, right? We've only seen three here in Samaria—Philip, Peter, and John. What about the other nine? Maybe they need a booking agent. Gotta keep the experiences coming... Ka-ching!

—Based on Acts 8:4-25

Experience is great and wonderful, and, as we've pointed out in the preceding chapters, even necessary for knowing the fullness of all God has for us.

But it's not an end in itself. It's not the point. A good friend and I were talking about how powerfully God had revealed himself in our church and all we saw Him doing in our midst. During the conversation he said, "We just need to get people into the presence of God and keep them there as long as we can. It would change their lives forever! Our goal should be to get them there as often as possible and keep them there as long as possible." Meaning that would make everything all better. Meaning all their problems would be gone or become insignificant. Heaven on earth.

He couldn't have been more wrong. Experience, while necessary, is not the be-all and end-all of Christianity. Experience, in and of itself, is incomplete. Insufficient. A rip-off. Remember, I said, "in and of itself."

Hey, wait a minute. Is this the same guy who wrote the preceding chapters I agreed so much with? Yes, still here. But while experience is necessary for knowing the fullness of all God has for us, experience itself is not the fullness of all God has for us. Let me say that again: Experience is necessary for knowing the fullness of all God has for us, but experience itself is not the fullness of all God has for us. Relationship with Jesus is.

Experience Is Not the Goal of Church

My friend was close. We do need to create an atmosphere where people can experience the presence of God. That's a necessary part of church. I think I was fairly clear about that in the preceding chapters. But it's not the goal of church.

In the fictitious story at the beginning of this chapter (based on the true story in Acts 8), Simon made experience an end in itself and never quite got it that the point is Jesus, not the experience of Him. It is a remarkably similar error to the opposite one discussed earlier, that of worshipping the Bible instead of the One who wrote it. By making experience an end in itself, we worship the experience instead of the One we're experiencing, and like that other error, it goes into idolatry.

Experience with the God of Heaven, the Lord of Hosts, can be idolatry? No, not the experience itself—but the worship of it, yes! Wanting to get back to the experience and the feeling, instead of longing to get back to God is idolatry.

There is a song that contains the line, "We seek Your face and not Your hand." Church should be coming to seek God's face. Period. That's all it is on our end. If we have any goals for church beyond that, we've got things messed up. God sets the goals for the church, not us. Our bit is just to seek Him out.

So we should not seek experience for its own sake—that's idolatry. But too often we come to church seeking God's hand. True, we desperately need His hand and His touch in our lives. But do we trust Him enough to say, "Although the circumstances of my life desperately need the touch of Your hand, I come to seek Your face." That requires trusting God that He'll deliver the touch we really need when we really need it, as opposed to the touch we think we need when we think we need it!

Experience Is Not the Evidence of Salvation

Need more proof that experience is incomplete? In the Sermon on the Mount, Jesus talked about many who will be rejected by Him when He returns to judge the world in spite of their tremendous experiences:

> *"Not everyone who says to me, 'Lord, Lord,' will enter the kingdom of heaven, but only he who does the will of my Father who is in heaven. Many will say to me on that day, 'Lord, Lord, did we not prophesy in your name, and in your name drive out demons and perform many mira-*

cles?' Then I will tell them plainly, 'I never knew you. Away from me, you evildoers!'" (Matthew 7:21-23)

They drove out demons, they performed many miracles, and I'm sure they had their share of shaking on the floor under the touch of almighty God, what some affectionately call "carpet time." But Jesus never knew them. They worshipped His power and His presence instead of worshipping Him. They were idolaters.

Experience Is Not the Anchor

For many Christians, their emotional experiences with God are the anchor of their faith. Experience is a natural consequence of a relationship with Jesus; indeed, it's the natural consequence of knowing Him (remember we don't really know what we don't experience). And it may be your own personal proof that God is real. But it's not what secures our salvation. It's not the cornerstone of our faith—Jesus is. Jesus and His redeeming blood should be the anchor of our faith. In fact, making experience the anchor, or foundation, of our faith starts sounding very much like Mormonism.

"What? You're comparing my anchoring my faith on my experience with almighty God to a cult experience?" Again, not the experience itself, only the part that we get out of balance—making that very necessary experience the anchor of our faith is very much like Mormonism.

The Latter-day Saints (Mormons) have an emotional experience they call "burning in the bosom" when they dedicate themselves to Mormonism. They are told that if ever they doubt the truth of what they've been taught, to remember and hold onto that "burning in their bosom" experience they had. They believe that experience was God confirming His truth to them. They are told that's the proof Mormonism is true, and they are to anchor themselves to that experience.

This demonic lie then sets them up to ignore all the logic, reason, and undeniable proof to the contrary. Very clever of Satan, in advance, to give his deceived an out when presented with the truth against Mormonism.

Experience Is Not God's Stamp of Approval

"But I must be right—I experienced Jesus!" Many Christians also fall prey to this trap. Because of some phenomenal experience they've had, they think they have a lock on perfect doctrine and stop listening to wise counsel from their pastors or other church leaders. They become unsubmissive and rebel against the spiritual authority God has placed over them. They create real problems in the church. Any pastor reading this knows exactly what I'm talking about.

Because of their awesome experiences with God, which are probably quite true and quite real, they think their pastor and even their whole church is somehow bound to accept whatever doctrine they're promoting. Especially if the awesome experiences happened while they were practicing their unbiblical doctrine.

In their pride, they think God gave them the experience as His stamp of approval on their doctrine and/or practices. They don't consciously realize it, but they really believe they've earned the experience because they were "doing it right." This is textbook self-righteousness.

They would be the first to deny this. "Doing it right" takes many subtle and sneaky forms. My favorite is, "We just want more of God," implying the people who disagree with them and all their unusual doctrines and practices don't want more of God and are just complacent.

This one is especially insidious because we all should continually want more of God, and many churches are complacent. But if we strive against our pastor because we think we have something figured out, neither our holy desire for God nor the church's complacency justifies our pride and rebellion against God's anointed authority in His church. In that case, I, the self-righteous one, need to repent before God's judgment falls on me!

It never occurs to these people that God granted them the experience of Himself out of His grace and mercy for them, simply because He loves them and wanted to bless them. It was all about His grace and not their doctrine! In fact, maybe they needed to experience the real God because they were getting so far out in left field that out of His mercy He's trying to bring them back!

So the very experience that is meant to bring repentance instead brings pride and rebellion because they do not allow themselves to be pastored through it. Instead, they try to pastor their pastor! They try to usurp the place, or we could say the authority that God has given their pastor. Hmmmm, wasn't there somebody, an angel or something, who tried to usurp a throne a very long time ago? (Look up Isaiah 14:13-15; Revelation 12:7-9; Luke 10:18 to see who I'm talking about if you haven't figured it out already.) God certainly did not provide the experience so we could follow that fallen angel's example!

Incomplete Experience

Let's look at all the things experience is not:

- NOT the goal of church
- NOT the evidence of salvation
- NOT the anchor of our faith
- NOT God's stamp of approval

Now these are all good things, and we need them. But our experience with God is not any of these things, and we get into trouble when we try to make it so.

Our emotional experience with God does not provide everything we need. Therefore, though necessary, it is incomplete. Not bad, but incomplete; not an end in itself, not the point. Jesus is always the point.

8

God's Eminent Domain

A False Doctrine of Happiness

Sadly, some Christians believe people's problems are because "they're not doing it right and/or they just need more of God." This is not always true. We say this because it makes pain easier to swallow. It's easier than believing undeserved bad things happen to good people.

It's much easier to believe that the woman whose baby died four hours after being born had a problem with pride or wouldn't receive the move of the Holy Spirit in her life. "I bet God has her attention now," we piously declare. That's much easier, much safer, than facing the truth that God sometimes does or allows things that appear horrific that we don't understand. "After all, if that were true, it could happen to me!" Yeah, and then we'd have to trust God for our security instead of the nice, neat, little cozy box we've all built around ourselves that God wants to demolish.

Why is it so important, especially for us in the West, to cling to this lie that bad things don't happen to good people?

And what do we mean by "good"? I'll tell you what we mean by "good"—we mean "us." We don't want to believe bad things, horrific things, can happen to us. We want to believe our experience with God will protect us from those things. Our experience with God will protect us *through* those things, not *from* them.

Really what we're saying is that we can protect ourselves from bad things happening to us by being good Christians and by experiencing God. Do you see how this is not trusting God? This subtle error takes God off the throne of our lives. The people who are free to openly experience God in church and in their private lives without having to hide it, who therefore should be the most gracious and understanding of all, become some of the most legalistic Pharisees in the Christian world because of their fear of suffering and over-developed desire for happiness.

How many times have we heard a parent say to an adult or adolescent child, or maybe even we said to our own children, "Honey, I just want you to be happy." In the movies, the sappy music's playing and we think, "What a great parent!" In reality, what a load of nonsense!

Since when did happiness become the goal of life? Jesus apparently didn't think so either. He said, "Woe to you who laugh now, for you will mourn and weep" (Luke 6:25). God never, anywhere in the Bible, promises us happiness. In fact, He promises us suffering: "In this world you will have trouble. But take heart! I have overcome the world" (John 16:33).

No, He doesn't promise us happiness—He promises us joy (Luke 2:10-11; John 15:11; 16:22; 17:13; Romans 14:17; 15:13; 1 Thessalonians 1:6; 1 Peter 1:8). And the two are different. Way different. Look up the above verses and see.

Happiness is situational. If everything is going fine, we're happy. If things go badly, we're not so happy. Jesus did not die on a cross so our state-of-being could be batted around randomly by external circumstances. He died on a cross to bring us to Himself and to give us joy—the inner peace that, in any situation, good or bad, Jesus is my God and it's going to be okay eventually, just maybe not on this side of paradise. God's joy, a side effect of His presence in our lives, makes us okay with that, even if we don't like it.

A True Doctrine of Suffering

God often brings unhappy experiences into our lives to increase our experiences with Him, our knowing Him, and to bless us by bringing us closer to Him. We pray, "O God, I want to experience You more. I want to be closer to You!" God may answer, "Granted. Over the next year I'll bring your eight-year-old daughter home to me. She's going to die of cancer, long and slow and painful. You and I will get very close."

We greet each other at church, "How are you?" "Oh, I'm fine, I'm so blessed. Everything in my life is just peachy." But we're not blessed. If we were blessed, God would bring some suffering into our lives so we could experience more of Him. Then we'd be blessed! See James 1:2-4:

> *Consider it pure joy, my brothers, whenever you face trials of many kinds, because you know that the testing of your faith develops perseverance. Perseverance must finish its work so that you may be mature and complete, not lacking anything.*

How about when we as parents say, "I just want my kids to have an easier life than I did." What nonsense! Do we want them to experience less of God? How foolish is that?

Granted, we want our kids to avoid suffering they bring on themselves. We want them to avoid sin and be wise. There is nothing wrong with that. But to wish them an easy life is just foolish and unrealistic because we know life's not easy. It just isn't. What we should be wishing, or better praying, is for them to know God—to experience Him deeply. Then we can have confidence that they will hide in Him and be safe through the suffering God brings into their lives for His own glory.

Problems and suffering in our lives should drive us to God. It's wise to run to Him during these times and not away from Him, as so many people foolishly do. But the problems, in and of themselves, do not necessarily mean we goofed up. They could be, and often are, the logical consequences of our own sin. But they might not be.

Eminent Domain

Believe it or not, our problems could actually be from God, a road into your life to pour out His power and His love. When a city or township decides to put a new road through, anybody who has the misfortune to own property in the way just loses it. It's commandeered by the government in a principle called eminent domain.

In the United States and most democracies, the government at least has to pay you for the land they take, but you don't have the choice not to sell it to them. It doesn't matter how many generations it's been in your family or what your emotional attachment is to it. In many other cultures, the government just takes it with no compensation at all. Anyone who's been to London knows which roads were built by the ancient Romans—the straight ones—for miles and miles dead-on straight. If the Roman army decided to put a road through and your farm was in the way, well, that was just too bad for you.

Do we grant Jesus eminent domain in our lives? Don't we all believe Jesus is the sovereign God of our lives? That He can do anything he wants? We all say we do, but then when He really does do anything He wants (especially without asking us or warning us first), we freak out. We flip out. We go ballistic. We go postal, verbally murdering anyone who has the misfortune to be in the path of our rampage.

Now we know who, or what, is really god in our life, and whether or not it's the real God. If it is the real God, we'd go straight to Him. And we wouldn't have to go far because we'd be living the whole day with Him, experiencing Him. We may go to Him quite emotional in the horror of the moment. That's fine, that's real, but there's always a quiet acceptance underneath it all that He really can do whatever He wants in our lives, and it's okay with us. We'll do it God's way and take the consequences—lose our jobs, lose some money, lose a friend, or lose our lives, and it's okay. As long as we don't lose Jesus.

Paul said, "I have learned the secret of being content in any and every situation" (Philippians 4:12). Have we? Or have we experienced so little of God that our contentment is still tied to our happiness?

Who Sinned?

Jesus' disciples were good legalistic Christians—they had

learned their lessons from their religious teachers, the Pharisees, quite well. So when they came to a man born blind (John 9:1-3), they asked Jesus (v. 2): "Rabbi, who sinned, this man or his parents, that he was born blind?" Somebody had to sin here—tragedies like this don't happen to righteous people like us.

But Jesus told them (v. 3): "Neither this man nor his parents sinned," said Jesus, "but this happened so that the work of God might be displayed in his life." Did you catch that? Jesus told them neither! Nobody sinned! His blindness wasn't the result of anybody's sin. This happened so that God's power could be displayed in his life. And then Jesus went on to display His power in the guy's life by healing him—God's eminent domain.

So, while the sin in our own lives will certainly create problems and consequences we have to deal with, not all problems or tragedy is associated with sin. It could actually be associated with righteousness.

The Eminent Domain Poster Child

Look at God exercising his eminent domain in Job's life! Job was a perfectly righteous man who pleased God (Job 1:1). Directly because of Job's righteousness (Job 1:8), God intentionally placed him in Satan's hands twice (Job 1:12; 2:6)! His oxen and donkeys were carried off by raiders (Job 1:14-15), fire from heaven burned up his sheep and servants (Job 1:16), his camels were carried off by different raiders (Job 1:17), and all his sons and daughters were killed in one mighty rush of wind that collapsed the house they were in (Job 1:18-19). As if that's not enough, he got painful sores all over his body (Job 2:7). Talk about a bad week!

His three buddies showed up and said what many Christians today would: "Job, you sinned! You didn't do it right!" His buddy Eliphaz says in Job 4:7, "Consider now: Who, being innocent, has ever perished? Where were the upright ever destroyed?"

False Prosperity Gospel

This gives rise to the popular teaching in some Christian circles that God wants us to be prosperous, meaning wealthy. Where did we read that? In the book of First Capitalism?

Sometimes, the innocent do perish, and the upright are destroyed. Remember the Holocaust? How about Stalin's purges? Ever been to China or a Muslim country under Sharia Law lately? Why does this happen? Why did God allow the horrific things to happen to Job? Or even here in America, when a three-year-old boy is killed in a drive-by shooting. So Job's problems weren't because Job wasn't doing it right or he just needed to experience more of God.

All this happened to Job for God's glory! This is a reason we really don't understand and certainly don't like. But Job's refusal to curse God brought God glory. Christians in China and Muslim countries who choose death and torture instead of denying Jesus bring glory to Him. And in God's eternal view, they don't perish and they're not destroyed, even though they give up their lives in this world (Matthew 10:39; Revelation 14:13). God repays one hundred times whatever we give up in this life (Matthew 19:29).

In his book *The Heavenly Man*, Brother Yun, a Chinese pastor who has experienced extremely violent torture and years of prison for being a Christian, says, "Don't pray that God removes our suffering from us. Then we'd become complacent like the West. Instead, pray for us that we might bear up under it."[1]

What? Don't pray that God rescues us from our suffering? This is from a guy who's had an electric cattle prod in his mouth on more than one occasion and had fasted for so long in prison his wife didn't recognize him.

Proverbs 21:1 says, "The king's heart is in the hand of the Lord; he directs it like a watercourse wherever he pleases." Quite frankly, in all problems we experience in our lives, whether the logical consequences of sin or not, God is doing just that, directing your heart, like the water in a canal, exactly where He wants it to go. Choose to go there. Let the river flow.

The Bottom Line Is Faith— What It Is and What It Isn't

Faith isn't trusting God that nothing bad will happen to us. It's recognizing that the bad stuff that does happen to us is a sacrifice He's calling us to make, the cross He's given us to bear.

What did Jesus say? "For whoever wants to save his life will lose it, but whoever loses his life for me will save it" (Luke 9:24). Ted Dekker makes the point in his *The Martyr's Song Series* novels that we Western Christians are too attached to our flesh, to our lives. And he's right. We view sacrifice as something to be avoided rather than as a means to "work out your salvation with fear and trembling" (Philippians 2:12). We preach a false doctrine of happiness, mocking the cross of Christ, and think faith is believing God for that happiness.

Mixed Emotions

To the contrary, faith is accepting the bad stuff, doing it His way, sticking with Him through the bad stuff. Even if it kills us or someone close to us. And it just might. But that's okay because worse things could happen—we might deny Jesus. That's faith. That's where the rubber meets the road—where our flesh meets the sacrifice.

Do we believe God or not? God knows all along—the times of suffering are when we get to find out. Talk about experiencing God—these are the times! Quite honestly, the experience and knowledge of God is for the bad times, not the avoidance of them.

God brings suffering into our lives for his glory and to draw us closer to him, not necessarily because of anything wrong in our lives.

So enough of this nonsense that all the pain in our lives, or someone else's life, is the result of not experiencing enough of God. Some of it probably is the logical consequence of sin. But some of it is not. It's God's eminent domain in our lives, steering our hearts where He wishes them to go, to bring glory to Himself.

And you know what? He even wants to do that with the pain in our lives that is the result of our own sin. He loves us that much.

[1] Yun, Brother with Paul Hattaway, *The Heavenly Man: The Remarkable True Story of Chinese Christian Brother Yun* (Grand Rapids, Mich.: Kregel, 2002)

9

A Pride Response

Sand. It's everywhere. Desert yesterday, desert today, desert tomorrow. Boring. Really boring. Boring, boring, boring. What's a young person to do for fun around here, anyway? As Aaron's two oldest sons, Nadab and Abihu, we're both kinda thinking the same thing.

I mean look, it's cool that we aren't slaves in Egypt anymore, and the way the Lord split the Red Sea for us but then drowned the whole Egyptian army was totally awesome. We got it in on our iPhones and had it uploaded to Facebook within the hour, dude. By the next day it had gone viral, and we were getting likes from Assyria to Persia.

But we've been out here in this desert in the Sinai peninsula wandering around for months eating nothing but manna and quail. I mean, dude, really, there's not even cell coverage out here. And the sand. Gets. Everywhere.

At least we're priests, so we have more to do than the average unemployed Israelite. But it's all so serious. Dad keeps calling us back for yet another fitting for the ephods and other priestly clothes the craftsmen are

Mixed Emotions

making for us. And Uncle Moe has been no fun at all since that whole golden calf thing. I mean, dude, the community got the lesson so get over it already.

But at least today is the day. We've already been camping out in front of the Tent of Meeting, where Dad and Uncle Moe meet with the Lord, for a week solid doing the whole priestly gig. This is the eighth day—the Big Assembly of all the people at the Tent of Meeting. Finally all the preparations are done, and today us priests officially start our ministry with a big Consecration Ceremony. Everyone'll see us helping Dad make the sacrifices. This is the big show. The pageantry! The grandeur! The spectacle! The sand—it's still everywhere.

The whole community shows up; it's kinda mandatory. But again—desert—not much else to do, so no one would miss it for the world. Uncle Moe gets things started telling the community, "This is what the Lord has commanded you to do, so that the glory of the Lord may appear to you." Then we begin making the sacrifices—Dad slaughters a calf first, as a sin offering for himself. We bring him the blood; some he puts on the altar's horns, and he pours the rest out at the base.

There are a lot more offerings to do—bulls, rams, goats, and an ox. It's fun but it's hard work. There's a lot to keep track of. We hand him the blood, which he sprinkles on the altar. We hand him the animal parts—some parts he burns on the altar, some parts he waves to the Lord, some parts get sent outside the camp to get burned up there. Some parts we get to eat; some parts we don't. Somehow we manage to keep it all straight. We have to get this stuff right or Uncle Moe gets real cranky. But we've been practicing all week so we got it down pretty well, if we do say so ourselves.

A Pride Response

After completing all the sacrifices, we're really beat. Except the main parts of the burnt offering are still on the altar unlit—what's up with that? Uncle Moe hasn't told us how or when that's getting lit—probably for a big finale.

Dad lifts his hands and blesses all the people. Then he and Uncle Moe pop into the Tent of Meeting to meet with the Lord. When they emerge, they bless the people again, and look at that—the glory of the Lord shining among the people! We're so caught up in the experience we don't even think of videoing this. But it doesn't matter, because it wouldn't do it justice anyway. There are no words in the language to describe what the glory of the Lord looks like, feels like, sounds like, smells like. And we are experiencing it—this is totally legit!

Wait, why are Dad and Uncle Moe moving away from the front of the Tent of Meeting so quickly? Whoa, dude, fire from the presence of the Lord in the Tent of Meeting shoots outside, nails the altar, and burns up the burnt offering! Did we just see that? Everyone's shouting for joy and falling on their faces before the Lord, including us. This is absolutely incredible!

Afterward, we're physically and emotionally exhausted. Wow, what a day! We plop down on beach chairs (sand, remember?) and start talking about the day.

"Well, that was epic."

"I know, right? It was pretty legit."

"Well, back to the boring. It was a great start, but it's gonna get pretty monotonous now. Sacrifice the bull. Sacrifice the goat. Sacrifice the ram. Repeat. And lighting everything ourselves from now on."

"Dude, we can do this whenever we want. We're priests, right? We got ephods just like Dad's. What's stopping us?"

"We could go do one right now! Let's go!"

"Do you think Dad and Uncle Moe'll yell at us for being presumptuous?"

"Nah. They'll be happy we're finally taking some initiative. We gotta repeat this experience."

We get back into our priestly dress blues and return to the tent of meeting. This is going to be so epic! Before anyone notices what we're doing, we put fire in our censors, add the incense, and offer it to the Lord. Then we wait to enjoy the show. Here it comes!

"Hey, Bro, is it getting a little warm out here to you?"

– *Based on Leviticus 9:1–10:3, where Aaron's sons were consumed by the fire of the Lord for offering unauthorized fire, being presumptuous in His presence.*

The wonderful experience we had with God was given to heal us, bless us, draw us closer to Him, etc. The fact that the God of the universe is touching us should humble us. But let's explore what happens when it gets all twisted around with our pride and puffs us up instead—when our focus and our message becomes our experience instead of God's grace.

Sometimes people start what some call "splinter group" meetings. Without the pastor's permission and often without even his knowledge, they have meetings at their houses to pursue the idol of their experience. Sometimes they even tell their pastor, "so-and-so are getting together at our house tonight if you want to come." But they neglect to tell him the whole story and are only mentioning it to get his token "okay," which they falsely believe means he blesses and covers the meeting. They comfort themselves because what they told him was honest—deceitfully honest! They didn't tell the whole truth, that they are having the meeting because they don't agree with his vision for the church and because he's not doing it right. So they're going to do it right themselves, and get what they can't get in church.

How arrogant could we be? And we expect God to bless this? "God opposes the proud but gives grace to the humble" (Proverbs 3:34; 1 Peter 5:5; James 4:6). He may show up in the short term out of grace for us, but if we don't repent he will start openly opposing us, and being opposed by God is never a pretty picture.

But we just want more of God. No, if we're doing this, we just want more of God's fireworks, His signs and wonders. Sure we're seeking His presence—the same way Herod sought Jesus' presence in order to see a miraculous sign (Luke 23:8). But what Jesus has to say about us and our pride and our rebellion, well, we're not open to that.

Holy Spirit Flambé

So these meetings take place without any pastoral covering. They are like the unauthorized fire Aaron's sons brought before the Lord. I dramatized Leviticus 9:1–10:2 at the beginning of this chapter from the point of view of Aaron's sons. Here's the real account: "Aaron's sons Nadab and Abihu took their censers, put fire in them and added incense; and they offered unauthorized fire before the Lord, contrary to his command. So fire came out from the presence of the Lord and consumed them, and they died before the Lord" (Leviticus 10:1-2).

Aaron's sons just wanted more of God. They thought they had a lock on doing it right. "Wow, the presence of God is awesome! We just need more of this. Let's help Moses and Aaron out by sharing the load and getting more of God!" Sounds reasonable enough. God didn't think so, though. They were out of order and presumptuous. And they got "Holy Spirit flambé" for their troubles.

God broke out against them and burned them alive. Crispy critters, they rebelled against the order and hence the authority God had established. They worshipped the presence instead of worshipping God. They came into His holy presence to worship His presence and His power instead of worshipping Him. Essentially, they were performing idolatry in His very presence—a bad move! Perhaps this explains God's strong response.

God gives a literal grace period for these splinter groups to repent, but if they don't repent, He will break out against them and their lives will become Holy Spirit flambé. Hopefully, they won't split their local church in the process.

Brilliant Demonic Strategy

If we think about it from Satan's point of view, it's a clever strategy: "Oh no! They're experiencing God! We can't have that! But we can't stop the Holy Spirit from moving, and hence we can't stop them from experiencing God, so we need to redirect it. Let's see, here . . . I know, get them to worship the experience! That'll do!" Actually, from Satan's point of view, worshipping anything will do except for God Himself. In fact, we can look at all sin as idolatry of some sort; that is, worshipping something other than God.

And then they've got us, hook, line, and sinker. People will go to fantastic lengths to defend their false gods. The strength that God put in us to be tenacious for Him, that was intended to martyr itself in defense of the one true God, gets twisted and all its energy put into dying and killing (spiritually) for a false god.

And just like the Mormons, people have a "godly" experience to fall back on when God uses others to confront them about their lives. Except with Christians, the deception is so much more powerful when it really was a God-blessed, God-ordained, true experience.

So we end up using the truth in our lives (the experience of God) to defend the falsehood in our lives (the issues God is wanting us to deal with). "How dare that pastor talk to me like that! He's never even experienced God like I have!" Can't you just feel the pride dripping off those words?

And the demons are rolling on the floor, laughing their heads off! It's so ridiculous that I'd be laughing too if this deception wasn't so tragically playing itself out over and over again in churches all across the "civilized" Christian world.

A Pride Response vs. a Humble Response

Too often when people have true experiences with God (I'm not even talking about the false ones), they respond with a pride response. They say, "Wow, through this experience God is empowering me to birth this into my church! I can't wait to take it back to my home church!" Translation: "I can't wait to tell my pastor how to do it right!" Believe it or not, God will birth His stuff into His church through our pastor—not through us! This thing may truly have come to us to take back to our church—but it'll still be birthed through our pastor—not through us!

We need to go to our pastor and respectively and humbly tell him about it, and let him pastor us through it. And then be patient and wait on God until God tells him what God wants him to do about it. It may take some time for both us and our pastor to figure it out. Although we may have gotten the revelation, our pastor has to seek out the interpretation, the application/wisdom, and the timing for the church as a whole. And believe it or not, our pastor knows more about where God is taking our particular church than we do. He may even decide the experience was just from God to us and not to pastor it to the church as a whole. And he might be right.

Why doesn't anybody ever say, "Wow, through this experience God is empowering me to become a greater servant to His Body and be more long-suffering and patient with people, and learn how to wash their feet!" Translation: "I can't wait to repent before my pastor and ask his forgiveness for trying to tell him what God should be telling him, for trying to be God to him!" That would be a humble response. You know I'm really not sure, but somehow I think our pastor might be a bit more receptive toward our experience if we had this attitude.

Let's apply this principle of humble response globally, to the body of Christ at large. Paul wrote in Romans 2:24, "As it is written, 'God's name is blasphemed among the Gentiles because of you.'" We could paraphrase this as, "Because of you Jews, the Gentiles hate God." We could apply this to today and say, "Because of the excesses and prideful attitudes of you who have emotional experiences with God, the rest of Christendom hates the presence of God!"

The rest of the Christian world might be just a tad more receptive to God experiences if we who have them didn't use them as a license for all sorts of unbiblical doctrine! And please stop telling people they aren't saved because they didn't have our experience! We need to get over ourselves.

Our Basis of Faith

What do we anchor our faith on? The Bible, of course, the Word of God, and more so on the fact that we know the Author, Jesus Himself, and have a relationship with Him. Also we anchor it on everything He has done for us, both on the cross and individually in our lives. Because Jesus did it and God said it. Period. End of discussion.

In those dark times of doubting that threaten your soul that we all must pass through, it comes down to whom you're going to believe: the depression that says you're worthless, or the Holy Spirit through the Bible that says you were bought with a price and are valuable to God (1 Corinthians 6:20; 7:23). Will you believe your pride and fear that says, "God will finally love me if I do this ministry"? Or will you believe the Bible that says God loved you before you were ever even saved, and nothing you do can make Him love you more because His love is based on sonship and daughtership, and is not something you have to earn (Romans 5:8; 8:15)?

The basis of our faith, even when things look insane and insurmountable, is saying, "I chose to believe God even though it doesn't make sense to me." Faith says, "Even though I'm terrified, I chose to believe God." As it says in 2 Corinthians 5:7: "We walk by faith, not by sight" (NKJV).

So the anchor, or basis, of our faith is the Bible, the Word of God, while the fullness of our faith, knowing God Himself, is found through experience.

We need to be careful not to get these two twisted round. So often Christians who rightfully love the Word, knowing the Word is the basis of faith, try to also make it the fullness of our faith, an end in itself, and so get caught up in idolatry. And equally often Christians who have a God experience, knowing experience leads to the fullness of our faith, try to anchor their faith on their experiences, which doesn't work either because then it also becomes idolatry.

The funny thing is (only it's not so funny) that both groups point to the other group's idolatry to justify their own, cutting the body of Christ in half with a chainsaw. Christians on both sides who would never watch the movie *The Texas Chainsaw Massacre* do the very same thing to the body of Christ for real—not with special effects but repeatedly with their tongues when they bad-mouth the other group and then pat themselves on the back for doing it right and for being so holy. And all the while the demons are laughing their heads off. They love horror movies, especially in church.

So our experience with God requires a humble response and not a pride response.

Starting up splinter groups, trying to force our experience on the rest of the church, or thinking that, because of our experience, we now have the mandate to tell our pastor how to do it right—these are all pride responses. They all over-emphasize the experience and under-emphasize Jesus, who was the point of the experience all along.

If we have a humble response, the majority of our story will be about Jesus and what He's doing in our lives and not about the details of our experience. If we mention them at all, it will be to point people to Jesus in the context of what He has done for us. But the emphasis is not on us (in the form of our experience), but on Jesus.

10

Down the Mountain

It was almost the end of Jesus' ministry, but the disciples didn't know that. He had just begun to teach them about his upcoming death and resurrection, but as usual they didn't get it at the time. He was talking to them through a time warp; He knew they wouldn't understand at the time, but the Holy Spirit would bring His words back to them in the future when they needed them, much the same way parents talk to children.

So, knowing He would die in Jerusalem at Passover, Jesus began an informal farewell tour, visiting everywhere He'd been one last time, although the disciples didn't know it. Caesarea Philippi. Capernaum. Galilee. Samaria. Judea. Bethany. And finally Jerusalem.

It was early in this final farewell tour, in a remote place between Caesarea Philippi and Capernaum that our story takes place. About a week earlier, Peter had just been highly praised and then severely rebuked by Jesus. Highly praised when he confessed Jesus was the Christ, the Son of the Living God, when Jesus had asked His disciples who they thought He was. Jesus said the Father had revealed this to Peter and changed his name on the

Mixed Emotions

spot from Simon to Peter, the Rock, and said that on this rock He would build His church. Peter was flying high for about ten minutes.

Then Peter was severely rebuked when he tried to convince Jesus he really didn't have to do this whole suffer and die thing because it didn't fit with the Savior persona.

Jesus yelled at him, "Get behind me, Satan! You're a stumbling block to me! You don't have in mind the things of God, but the things of men!"

Peter's head was still reeling, trying to reconcile these two seemingly contradictory experiences, when Jesus called him, James, and John to take a walk with Him up a mountain. Just the four of them.

When they reached the top, Jesus got all white and shiny. He and His clothes and face all became white as light. And suddenly Moses and Elijah, just as shiny, were standing there talking with Jesus about the salvation He was about to accomplish when He returned to Jerusalem.

Score! They had arrived! Experiencing Jesus in all His glory. Oh. My. Word. This was it. No need to go any further. Just stay right here. In this experience. Forever.

So Peter, recovering quicker than the others and his own brain, walked right up and said to Jesus, "Lord, it's great to be here! Let's put up three tents, one for you, one for Moses, and one for Elijah, and we'll all just stay right here. Yes!"

But while he was still speaking, a cloud suddenly covered them all, and the voice of Father God said, "This is My Son, whom I love, with Him I am well pleased. Listen to Him!" Needless to say, Peter, James, and John hit the deck in terror. Nobody got in a cloud with God that close and lived to tell about it.

Down the Mountain

But Jesus tapped them on the shoulder. "It's alright, don't be afraid. Get up. Let's head back down." When they looked up, they saw only Jesus, looking normal again. No Moses, no Elijah, no cloud, no voice. And then, on the way down, Jesus told them not to tell anybody.

Ah, man, thought Peter. *We can't tell anybody. I was so looking forward to rubbing this in Andrew's face. What is the deal, anyway? Why couldn't we stay on the mountaintop? We had it made up there—Jesus in his glory! What's better than that? Everything else will seem rather dull now in comparison.*

When they got back down to the valley, they discovered the other nine disciples had gotten themselves into a bit of a pickle. They were trying to cast a particularly stubborn demon out of a little boy, and they just couldn't do it. Jesus, of course, did it easily.

That night, Peter couldn't sleep. He was chewing on all this. He still wished they hadn't come down the mountain. *I mean, my gosh, after what we just saw, how could Jesus possibly expect us to return to the ordinary?* But on the other hand, if they hadn't, that precious little boy would still be tortured by that nasty demon.

Then a thought occurred to him that he'd never thought before. *What if it wasn't about him? I mean, what about Jesus? If that's the glory He had with His Father before He came here, how could He ever lay that all down to come to live with us—the poorest of the poor, in an oppressed, occupied little country?*

But Jesus did leave it all, all the glory, the ultimate mountaintop, and here He is with us. So what if the purpose of the mountaintop experience wasn't to stay on the mountaintop? What if the purpose of the mountaintop experience was to enable mountaintop living in the valley

and to pass it on to other valley dwellers? After all, isn't that what Jesus spent the last two and half years doing?
— *Based on Matthew 16:15–17:18*

Experience is not an end in itself, not even a phenomenal experience like the transfiguration. There is a purpose to it. God gives the experience for a reason. Let's look at some examples.

Paul's Experience and His Sufferings

The apostle Paul had an awesome experience with God. It knocked him off his horse, literally—the resurrected Jesus actually spoke to him and called him by name (Acts 9:1-30). This experience changed his life. He went from persecuting the gospel to preaching it.

Why did God give this awesome experience to Paul? What did God want to show him? How cool it is to flop 'n' bop on the dusty road in the presence of Jesus? So he could "wow" all his friends by telling them about the experience and feel good about himself? Just to tickle Paul and show him how much his heavenly Santa Claus loves him?

No, the reason is given by God Himself in Acts 9:16: "I will show him how much he must suffer for my name."

God gave Paul this awesome experience because he knew Paul was going to need it. In 2 Corinthians 11:23-27, Paul recounts everything he has suffered for Jesus' name:

- Prison
- Five times whipped one lash from death
- Three times beaten with rods

- Stoned
- Three times shipwrecked
- A night and a day floating in the open sea
- Danger from rivers
- Danger from bandits
- Danger from Jews
- Danger from Gentiles
- Danger in the city
- Danger in the country
- Danger at sea
- Danger from false brothers
- Gone without sleep
- Hungry and thirsty
- Cold and naked

He didn't mention, because they hadn't happened yet at the time he wrote 2 Corinthians, another shipwreck, a long imprisonment, several assassination attempts, and finally being beheaded in Rome.

The awesome experience Paul had on the road to Damascus did not get him through all this. His relationship with Jesus did. An angel appeared to Paul at one point to strengthen him (Acts 27:23) because the Damascus road experience itself wasn't enough. Knowing Jesus got him through all he suffered. And that relationship was set up by God with the experience on that Damascus road.

So God gave Paul the awesome experience, not as an end in itself but to set up a relationship with Himself that God knew Paul would need and rely on the rest of his life. There was a point to the experience.

Paul's Vision and the Thorn in His Flesh

Paul had another experience with God, arguably even more awesome than the Damascus road experience. We only know about it because Paul obscurely mentions it in 2 Corinthians.

To give you the background, Paul planted the church in Corinth, considered the people his children, and suddenly they demanded proof that the Holy Spirit was really speaking through him. After all, Paul didn't do as many miracles or have as many visions as these other guys claim they've done and had, these traveling "super-apostles" who are greatly confusing the Corinthians and leading them away from Paul's solid teaching (2 Corinthians 13:3; 11:5, 13).

This was a very painful time for Paul. He changed his plans and delayed a scheduled trip to Corinth in order to spare both them and himself a painful visit. Instead, he sent Titus to them with the letter of 2 Corinthians. It's a very personal letter, and in it he defends his ministry to those whom he shouldn't have to defend it. He hoped this letter would prepare their hearts for his visit so that it would be blessed rather than painful (2 Corinthians 1:15-17, 23-2:2; 13:1, 10).

These false super-apostles are boasting about all they've done and experienced. This seems to be what the Corinthians want and are impressed by, so Paul will boast too, even though he thinks it's insane, and he says he's out of his mind to talk like this (2 Corinthians 11:1, 16-17, 23; 12:1, 11).

It's in this context that Paul talks about an amazing vision he received from the Lord. He's so reluctant to talk about it he doesn't even ascribe it to himself: "This guy I know had this vision..." Let's pick it up in 2 Corinthians 12:1.

I must go on boasting. Although there is nothing to be gained, I will go on to visions and revelations from the Lord. I know a man in Christ who fourteen years ago was caught up to the third heaven. Whether it was in the body or out of the body I do not know—God knows. And I know that this man—whether in the body or apart from the body I do not know, but God knows—was caught up to Paradise. He heard inexpressible things, things that man is not permitted to tell. I will boast about a man like that, but I will not boast about myself, except about my weaknesses (2 Corinthians 12:1-5).

Talk about an incredible experience! The guy was caught up to heaven with God, and heard the secret things of God, things he's not even allowed to repeat! Why did God give him such an awesome experience and then not even let him talk about it?

Paul's experience is connected to the suffering he was to undergo for the kingdom of God. Let's continue with verse 7:

To keep me from becoming conceited because of these surpassingly great revelations, there was given to me a thorn in my flesh, a messenger of Satan, to torment me. Three times I pleaded with the Lord to take it away from me. But he said to me, "My grace is sufficient for you, for my power is made perfect in weakness." Therefore I will boast all the more gladly about my weaknesses, so that Christ's power may rest on me (2 Corinthians 12:7-9).

It's clear Paul's incredible experience with God was connected to his suffering for the kingdom.

What is this "thorn in my flesh" he was talking about? We're not sure, but most scholars believe it has something to do with his eyes being infected, swollen, and filled with pus all the time. There is support, though not proof, for this theory in Scripture. Remember his Damascus road experience? He was blinded for three days afterward while he fasted and prayed (Acts 9:9). Then the Lord sent a believer named Ananias to Paul to pray for him, and Paul's blindness was healed (Acts 9:10-19).

Acts 9:18, when Ananias prayed and Paul received his sight back, says, "Immediately, something like scales fell from Saul's eyes, and he could see again." So there was some physical impediment with his vision. The traditional view is that his eyes remained a problem for him the rest of his days.

Support for this is found at the end of Galatians, in Galatians 6:11: "See what large letters I use as I write to you with my own hand!" Large letters? What is he talking about? Because he had such trouble seeing, he dictated his letters to someone else to write down, except for a personal blurb at the end. So the "large letters" means the individual characters he writes himself, because he has such trouble seeing (Romans 16:22; 1 Corinthians 16:21; Colossians 4:18; 2 Thessalonians 3:17).

So anybody want to look the apostle Paul in the face and tell him his thorn in the flesh is the result of his sin? Or that he just needs more of God? Or that he's not doing it right? His suffering was the direct result of his experiencing God in possibly one of the most awesome visions God has ever given anyone. Paul starts verse 7 with, "To keep me from becoming conceited…" So his suffering was actually God's grace to him to keep him from sin—namely, conceit.

For Paul, his experiences were never an end in themselves; they were never the point. Jesus always was. That's a good enough example for me. How about you?

The Transfiguration

Now we come to the example this chapter was named after—Jesus' transfiguration. When Jesus was here on earth, His glory was cloaked except once. Once, just for a moment, He let what He really looks like sneak out but only to His closest friends.

The transfiguration is the story of that "once," and I dramatized it at the beginning of this chapter. It's covered in Matthew 17, Mark 9, and Luke 9.

If experience is an end in itself, if we just need to get in the presence of God and stay there as long as we can, then Peter had the right idea, didn't he? Jesus in his glory—it doesn't get any better than that! "Thanks for bringing us here, Jesus, we've arrived, we'll just stay right here on top of this mountain, thank you very much. Let's pitch our tents and stay right here!"

Often we want to do just that. Stay on top of the mountain. Put up shelters to house our experiences so we can come back and visit them often. After all, that's the point, isn't it? To stay in that place as long as we can?

No, not quite. That's not the point. You see, Jesus led them back down the mountain according to God's plan. The rest of the disciples, a harried father, and a young boy were having a very difficult time down there in the valley below.

Why do we want to stay on the mountaintop? Have we

no discernment? Having spent time experiencing Jesus, do we not have His heart? There are people down in the valley in bondage, dying, and Jesus wants to heal them, set them free, minister to them, and deliver them! Do we have His heart for them? Or do we just want our spiritual warm fuzzies?

Notice also that they (Peter, James, and John) told no one what they had seen. They didn't come down and say, "Hey guys, you've got to come with us back up this mountain! Boy, have we got a show for you! You've got to experience this—it will change your life!"

No, Jesus ordered them not to tell anyone what they'd seen until after His resurrection. Why? Because after His resurrection, they'd get the Holy Spirit, which they'd need to understand the interpretation, the application/wisdom, and the timing—the point of the revelation! Before then, they would just get it all turned around. Case in point: the very next verse, Mark 9:33, they are arguing about who's the greatest!

Jesus wisely didn't want them talking about their experience before they received the Holy Spirit and could properly understand it. They would turn it into a doctrine, give themselves a badge for it, and puff themselves up. Build a ministry around it, Transfiguration Ministries, and solicit tax-deductible donations to take others less fortunate up the mountain to see the show. And they'd get it way, way, way, out of whack. "Come up the mountain, it will change your life!" It? Not Jesus?

Here's a free hint: anytime we as Christians say "it" instead of "Jesus," we're getting something out of whack, out of balance. We're getting into idolatry—worshipping God's presence rather than worshipping God.

Down the Mountain

So after they got the Holy Spirit, did the eye witnesses, Peter, James, and John, mention it? What did it do for them? Well, James never got the chance—Herod killed him with the sword, and he was the first apostle to be martyred (Acts 12:1-2). Peter mentions it briefly, vaguely, and in passing just so his readers know they're getting first-hand information:

> *We did not follow cleverly invented stories when we told you about the power and coming of our Lord Jesus Christ, but we were eyewitnesses of his majesty. For he received honor and glory from God the Father when the voice came to him from the Majestic Glory, saying, "This is my Son, whom I love; with him I am well pleased." We ourselves heard this voice that came from heaven when we were with him on the sacred mountain* (2 Peter 1:16-18).

What about John? He wrote five books in the New Testament including a gospel—does he ever mention it? Nope. After experiencing firsthand Jesus' glory, does he write about "it" at all? Nope, not one word. He writes about Jesus; he writes about love, which was the same thing to John because His relationship with Jesus was so deep.

If experience is such an end in itself, why is John the only gospel to not cover the transfiguration? Matthew, Mark, and Luke all cover it. They thought it was hot stuff. It certainly proves Jesus is God and shows Him as He really is. But of all four gospel writers, John was the only one who was actually there—why didn't he include it in his own gospel?

That's a good question. If experience is to be pursued above all else, why didn't John record the most awesome experience of his life in his own gospel? You can't get any more awesome than seeing Jesus in His glory—not in a vision but physically being there! As awesome as that experience was, it was not an end in itself for John. For whatever reason, it didn't fit into the point John was trying to make in his gospel so he left it out. His gospel was about Jesus, not about himself.

In fact, John refers to himself in his own gospel as "the disciple whom Jesus loved" (John 21:20; 13:23; 19:26; 21:7). What? Not the disciple who saw Jesus in His glory? Not the Son of Thunder, as Jesus called John and his brother James (Mark 3:17)? But no, he describes himself based on his relationship with Jesus, not his experience with Jesus, as "the disciple whom Jesus loved." Think about that.

Both Peter and Paul reference their experiences only occasionally and only to point to what Jesus did in their lives as part of their testimony. The experience you've had with God is part of your testimony. But we can't stay in the experience—we'd never have anybody to share our testimonies with!

So what was the point of the transfiguration experience on that mountain? Let's look at the broader context. It is right after Jesus teaches His disciples about denying themselves, taking up their cross, and following Him (Mark 8:34), and right before teaching them "the Son of Man is going to be betrayed" (Mark 9:30-31). So it is right in the middle of Jesus teaching them about both their suffering and His. Why do you suppose Jesus reveals Himself as He really is in the middle of a season of teaching His disciples about impending suffering?

Maybe He did so because they were going to need to know who He is to get through the suffering He wanted them to undergo. Peter was crucified upside down, James was the first disciple to be martyred, and John was exiled on a miserable, backward, little island. Maybe they needed the relationship with him that experience facilitated.

So experience is not an end in itself. There's a point to it. God gives experience for a reason. When we have such an experience, we should then pray (and pray, and pray, and then pray some more) to find out what that reason is. And God (usually!) will tell us. He's just waiting for us to ask, waiting for us to seek Him out. You may clearly be told what the point is or you may not, but either way you're getting closer to Jesus, and that is fruit no one can argue with.

The more time you spend with someone, the more they reveal themselves to you and you to them (intentionally or not). So experience with God is really just greater revelation of Him, the logical consequence of time spent.

Remember, with all revelation there's also interpretation, application/wisdom, and timing. Don't be so thrilled by the experience that you forget to ask God about the other phases and what the point is, and so rob yourself of the fullness and completeness of everything God wanted to do through that wonderful experience. He is excited about dialoging with you about that experience and teaching you new things out of it.

11

A Humble Response

All Satan really has to tempt us with are wrong motivations. He cannot undo or remove what God has done and is doing in our lives; he can only try to misdirect it. In Luke 4:1-13, Satan tempted Jesus with three wrong motivations:

- Meet his own needs, or some other "good" cause
- Give himself fame and the resulting platform
- Accomplish his mission through human strength and power

And all three come down to this: Who was Jesus living for—Himself or the Father? The answer to that question made all the difference in His responses to Satan's false and deceptive motivations.

Let's explore more deeply our inner motivations behind correct and incorrect responses to having an experience, emotional or otherwise, with God. It all comes down, ultimately, to who's sitting on the throne of your life. Whose mission are we on?

A Humble Response

Living for Ourselves

So now I've had this wonderful experience with God, and because I'm the one that had it, I know how awesome it was. And it blessed me so much I'm convinced everyone else needs it. Cringe, here's where we get into trouble. Our experience becomes a theology we impose on everyone else—a club with which to bludgeon the rest of the church. We have seen that God gives experience for a reason; I somehow doubt that was it.

"But we just want more of God," we say while refusing to let our pastor mature our experience. As if we had a right to it, and "Who is he to say anything to us?" Oh, I don't know, our pastor maybe—the God-given spiritual authority over us, charged by God to shepherd us by speaking truth into our lives even when it's uncomfortable truth and not what we want to hear.

When we get like this, we refuse God's blessing because we refuse the truth in which it was wrapped. Jesus speaks truly when He says about us, "Look, your house is left to you desolate. For I tell you, you will not see me again until you say, 'Blessed is he who comes in the name of the Lord'" (Matthew 23:38-39). Our pastor is the one "coming in the name of the Lord" whom we are not blessing by accepting what he has to say.

I may have stretched that verse a bit, but the principle still applies. If we reject our pastor's counsel instead of accepting and hence, blessing it, we shouldn't wonder later why our houses (lives) are decimated and desolate.

It's really the ultimate selfishness, thinking that everyone else needs my experience. It's another one of these brilliant demonic strategies. Every experience is personal and different

Mixed Emotions

so imposing ours on everyone else is doomed to fail because while it was God for us, it won't be God for everyone else. It was God for us because it was so personal, and it is exactly for that reason it won't be God for everyone else!

To quote Brother Yun again, from the book *The Heavenly Man*, he attempts to answer a question Western Christians often ask him, "Why is the Chinese church experiencing such great revival but not the churches in the West?"

An excerpt from his answer is, "When God moves in the West, it seems you want to stop and enjoy His presence and blessings too long, and build an altar to your experiences." Ouch.

So who are we living for here? Ourselves or God? When our experiences become the focal points of our walks with Jesus, when the ultimate goal of Christianity is to maximize our own personal experiences, then it has become all about us. At that point we're living for ourselves, not for God, and we are worshipping ourselves and our own pleasures.

We are no different than the materialistic people of the world who blow off God and live for their own pleasure and entertainment. But we look down our noses at them because our pleasures are "spiritual." Meanwhile, the demons laugh their heads off, and the Holy Spirit can't tell the difference.

Calm down before you start throwing things. Let me explain that last statement. What I mean is that the Holy Spirit of God does not differentiate between our worship of our "Christian" pleasures and materialists worship of their pagan pleasures, even though we do and are always happy to explain it at length to anyone unfortunate enough to ask.

But it's all idolatry to the Holy Spirit. The skin may be different (one looks spiritual on the outside while the other certainly doesn't), but the part the Holy Spirit of God is looking at, the heart, is the same. Identical. Worship of me and what I want and what I want now.

God has always cared about the inside, the heart. As he said to Samuel, when Samuel was trying to figure out which of Jesse's sons was to be the next king of Israel, "The Lord does not look at the things man looks at. Man looks at the outward appearance, but the Lord looks at the heart" (1 Samuel 16:7).

In one of his more frank moments (not that he was ever that subtle) Jesus said, "Woe to you, teachers of the law and Pharisees, you hypocrites! You clean the outside of the cup and dish, but inside they are full of greed and self-indulgence. Blind Pharisee! First clean the inside of the cup and dish, and then the outside also will be clean" (Matthew 23:25-26).

You're comparing us, those who have experienced Jesus so mightily, to the teachers of the Law and the Pharisees, the people who killed Him? Well, think about that. Jesus said they were full of greed and self-indulgence. If our experience has become an end in itself, then aren't we pursuing it for what we're going to get out of it? So the goal is what we're going to get. Hmmmm, isn't that greed by definition? Is the point of Christianity supposed to be what we get out of it? I don't think so.

If we're "practicing the presence of God" only because it feels good and we like it, isn't that just self-indulgence by definition? Is that what church is supposed to be? No. Now granted, sometimes the presence of God does feel good and we do like it, and that's fine, but that is not the reason we go into the presence of God or long for it.

There's that word "it" again! We shouldn't be longing for

"it," we should be longing for Jesus—and not because He makes us feel good about ourselves and gives us warm, secure, fuzzy feelings, but because we love Him. Just that simple. We love Him, long for Him, see only Him, and the rest of the whole world can just fade away. Oh, may we get to the point where we are ruined for this world!

Note that above I said "sometimes the presence of God does feel good"—but the presence of God doesn't feel so good when He's talking to us about our sin, whoops, I mean our "issues." Then it can get downright uncomfortable and unpleasant! Splinter groups don't typically address sin unless it is the rest of the church's sin—the other people's sin—never their own. After all, they have a lock on "doing it right."

Some Christians can spot this fallacy a mile away because they know the Word so well. And hence they want (correctly) nothing to do it or (incorrectly) any other emotional experience. Sometimes we who have had awesome experiences make it easy for other Christians to throw the baby out with the bath water.

If we are coming for the presence of Jesus instead of coming for just Jesus Himself, then like the teachers of the Law and the Pharisees, our hearts have become full of greed and self-indulgence.

Indeed, if our experience, or experiencing something in general, has become an end in itself, if our experience has become a doctrine that we impose on the rest of the body of Christ, then haven't we become teachers of that doctrine? Haven't we become teachers of doing it right? Haven't we become teachers of the Law? Think about that.

In that event, how can the next logical step be anything

other than rejecting the Son of God and killing Jesus all over again, just like they did? We don't kill Him by physically hanging Him on a cross like they did, but we kill His Body by splitting it in two. We're splitting the church or leaving it if we're in the minority. Or if we're in the majority, we're spiritually murdering (that is, getting them to leave) anyone who has the gall to even imply we might be getting things out of balance. Either way, we've killed the Son of God all over again, grieved the Holy Spirit, and stopped dead in its tracks what God wanted to do in our lives and in our church.

That's the logical, unavoidable result of living for ourselves, for our pleasures, be they pagan or spiritual—crucifying the Son of God all over again.

Living for God

Jesus said, "If anyone would come after me, he must experience my presence in ever increasing measure." What? Did I misquote that verse just a tad? Look it up, it's in Mark 8:34. See, we could handle it just fine if it really said that. We are so devoted to God, we would make a whole industry out of the "measure" part, so we could be sure it is "ever increasing." Books about "how to measure the presence of God" and "how to make sure it's ever increasing" would abound.

We'd even have God-O-Meter apps on our iPhones to track and trend the "ever increasing measure" of the presence of God in our lives! Then computer geeks like me would write other programs to fake-out the God-O-Meter software, giving it what it's looking for in a high score so we could peg the numbers and spend less time at it—being more efficient for the kingdom!

What does Mark 8:34 really say? "If anyone would come

after me, he must deny himself and take up his cross and follow me." That one won't sell so well. That verse slipped out of heaven without the approval of marketing. We'd rather go back to the "God is love" part of the Bible.

Let's take this verse apart and unpack it. "Deny himself." What does that mean? It means dying to what I want. My way. My "right" way. That's really hard. I can die to my personal preferences; although I like them, I'm not emotionally attached to them. But my "right" way? That's hard. We don't think we usually take a stand over something simply because it's our personal preference; we think we're taking a stand because it's the "right" way. But this verse is saying to give it up, let it go, lay down your weapons and back off of your stand, and erase your line in the sand.

"But then the other side will win! We'll have these consequences!" Is it really about us winning? How about we try a little experiment and let God deal with the consequences just for once? Ridiculous, isn't it? About as ridiculous as letting someone who has hit you on one cheek hit you on the other one also, like Jesus said to do in Matthew 5:39.

In fact, let's look at that verse. Jesus said, "But I tell you, Do not resist an evil person. If someone strikes you on the right cheek, turn to him the other also." Usually when we study this verse at all we skip to the last part and try to spiritualize and theorize what turning the other cheek really means so we don't actually have to do it. But there's no escaping the first part of the verse, "Do not resist an evil person." What? That's downright un-American! Yeah, I know, it really is—this "don't resist an evil person" thing is really hard for us since resisting and opposing evil is central to who we are as Americans.

Note that resisting evil and resisting an evil person are two different things. We should all be involved politically, both locally and nationally, to oppose the evil in our society and to support the good. But not resisting an evil person is speaking of our day-to-day dealings with the people around us. That means we let them win even when we know they are wrong. Again, not on a political level, but on a personal level. And not necessarily in every single situation but as a general pattern in our lives.

If we as Christians actually did this, put down our weapons, put down our point-of-view, turned the other cheek, did not resist evil persons but instead found some way to serve them, stopped guarding the artificial lines in the sand we all draw, and backed off our stands against each other, the surrounding society would notice because we'd actually be different. And guess what? It would give credibility to what we are preaching about evil in general in the society. But instead we have no credibility because while we preach something different than the surrounding society, we act exactly the same.

Dying to yourself. Denying yourself. The bottom line is, if we are honest with ourselves, we just can't. It doesn't even make sense to us. We need Jesus. How about it? Will you lay your weapons and your point-of-view down at the foot of the cross? Will you ask Him to take it, to enable you to lay them down?

What's the next part of Mark 8:34? "Take up his cross and follow me." What's that mean? Isn't it enough I've died to myself? Hey, don't complain to me. I don't like it either. It's not like I can do it. Jesus said it, whine to Him. But what does this mean? It means self-sacrifice versus self-indulgence—the very opposite of what we often do with our God-given experiences of Him!

This isn't a one-time event. It is a continuing action. Jesus is talking about a lifestyle here—a lifestyle of self-sacrifice, of serving, of living for others, of considering others better than ourselves. We need to consider them more deserving than us and smarter than us. "Oh now wait a minute, you're going too far here!" Am I? Read Philippians 2:3: "In humility consider others better than yourselves."

"So am I supposed to be a doormat?" We are supposed to live a life of love toward each other instead of a life of policing each other and managing each other's sins. In fact, we're not even supposed to notice each other's sins: "Love covers over a multitude of sins" (1 Peter 4:8). "Like that'll ever happen! Have you ever been to my church?" Maybe your church needs a couple more doormats.

Here's a new concept: How about I let my pastor deal with other people's sins and assume that he is. And, if I want to be really spiritual, how about I let my pastor deal with mine?

Maybe we should try to "out-doormat" each other, try to out-serve each other (Ephesians 5:21). Not to knock one of my favorite television shows, *Survivor*, but that would be better than trying to "outplay, outwit, and outlast" each other, seeing who gets voted out of the church at the next congregational meeting.

So what do you say? Is this Jesus you've just experienced so deeply and powerfully worth dropping your point of view and laying down your weapons? If you've experienced the same Jesus I have, I think you'll say yes.

Our experiences with Jesus, emotional or otherwise,

should bring us to a place of greater humility and servitude, not to a place of pride and spiritual superiority.

If others don't embrace, accept, and believe our experiences the way we hoped they would, it's often because they are picking up on our spiritual elitism. We think we're all that. But other people, including our pastor, know better and aren't fooled, even if we're fooling ourselves.

But instead, if our experiences make us humbler and greater servants, and give us a tendency to have more grace toward other people, those other people will be much more likely to accept the experiences we've had as something truly from God. It may even begin to be a blessing to them as well.

12

Really Knowing

"How dare they claim this dead heretic, Jesus from Nazareth in Galilee of all places, is the Messiah? I dragged them out of their beds in Jerusalem and into prison, and I will do the same to them in Damascus. I have letters from the chief priests in Jerusalem giving me the authority. We ride there now!

"I am envious of their confidence in their false Messiah, even to the point of their death, and I hate them all the more for it. But what do they know? Taught by a bunch of unrighteous fisherman and tax collectors!

"But I, Saul of Tarsus, will boast of my own faultless legal righteousness as I have good reason for such confidence! An Israelite of Israelites, of the tribe of Benjamin, circumcised on the eighth day according to the law of Moses, a Hebrew of Hebrews, and a Pharisee of Pharisees! Of this I have a right to be proud," I exhort my companions as we ride along. My righteousness will certainly spur their zeal!

Nathan interrupts me, "Look, Saul, we're almost to the city gate!"

"Quiet, Nathan, I'm monologuing!" I retort.

Really Knowing

"You don't have to be rude," Nathan mumbles under his breath.

I continue to inspire them: "I have sought hard my own advancement among the Pharisees and have advanced further than any of my contemporaries! My anger was easily aroused by these heretics, and I shall keep a record of every one of their wrongs! I delight in seeing them arrested and will never rejoice in their heresy.

"Alas, that we cannot always protect our people from such heretics! Our trust in our Sadducee leaders fades and our hope diminishes under every stroke of the Roman lash. We cannot always persevere, and sometimes we fail, but always . . ."

Right in the middle of my big finale a most inconvenient thing happens. Lightening all around us on a perfectly clear and sunny day! The thunder booms simultaneously and my horse throws me to the ground and bolts. I land flat and hard with a thud that knocks the wind out of me. And still this light is everywhere, even when I close my eyes! I can't see anything else!

"Saul, Saul, why do you persecute me?" says a voice from all around me—a voice like I'd never heard before like a mighty waterfall or rushing river.

"Who are you, Lord?" I ask rather sheepishly.

"I am Jesus, whom you are persecuting," replies the voice. Now this is awkward.

"Get up and go into the city, and I will tell you what to do," the voice continued. "I have appeared to you to appoint you as my servant and my witness to what I have shown you and will show you."

The light never goes away and it's all I can see. Don't blind people see just blackness? But my blindness is dif-

Mixed Emotions

ferent. All I can see is white light everywhere, even when I close my eyes. My companions find me and lead me by the hand into the city.

It's been three days here in Damascus, at the house of Judas on Straight Street. Nathan is trying to encourage me to eat. Again. "Saul, smell this fresh, hot bread!" But I just push it away. "At least drink something. It's been three days. You're weak, and you look terrible." He puts a cup of clear, cold water to my lips, but I turn my head and refuse to drink.

"Nathan, thank you for all you've done for me and all you're trying to do. You're a good friend," I tell him. "But I can't eat or drink until the Lord Jesus restores my sight. He told me so."

"Yeah, yeah," he says in frustration as he continues in his Australian accent, "and some bloke we don't even know named Ananias is going to come, somehow find us, pray for you, and restore your sight. Right. You've been telling us that for three bloody days, mate!"

"The Lord Jesus showed me in a vision," I remind him gently.

"In a vision!" He throws up his hands in frustration. "And will you stop talking about 'the Lord Jesus' for heaven's sake? Those nut jobs are the bad guys, remember? Dead heretic from Nazareth in Galilee of all places, letters from the chief priests, going to drag them back to Jerusalem to stand trial . . . Any of this ringing a bell?"

I pray silently for Nathan, that the Lord Jesus would open his eyes as well.

"Look," Nathan continues, "you had a nasty fall there off your horse, and you landed really hard. It's understandable you're shaken up a bit. It was just some really

Really Knowing

bright lightening on a completely clear, sunny day..." he trails off. "I admit that's a bit hard to explain, alright? Maybe it was just a reflection off the Roman's shields up on the city wall or something. But, look, we don't know anyone here in this whole city named Ananias."

"The Lord Jesus will bring him here," I say softly but confidently.

"Well, apparently 'the Lord Jesus' has trouble reading a map. It's been three bloody days, mate! Where is this Ananias bloke anyway?"

There's a loud knock at the door. "Judas," calls Nathan, "get the door, will ya? I'm trying to talk some sense into him."

After a moment, Judas comes in with a stranger, and says in his Southern drawl, "Um, Nathan, this here's somewhat awkward. This here fella's name is Ananias, and he's here to pray for Saul, to restore his sight."

I would give anything to not be blind and see Nathan's face at this moment. Priceless!

After Ananias prays for me and scales or something fall off my eyes and I can see normally again, he tells me, "Saul, I must admit I was more than a little afraid of coming here and seeing you after everything I heard about in Jerusalem. But the Lord told me, and I think you should know, that you are His chosen instrument to carry His name before the Gentiles and their kings and before the people of Israel. And He said He will show you how much you must suffer for His name."

I thank and embrace Ananias. We part as friends, no, as dear brothers—I, who rode here with hatred in my heart for him and all the brothers; and he, who knows this and still extends the hand of friendship and brotherhood to me.

Mixed Emotions

How shall I respond to my Lord, who in love revealed Himself to me, took off all my hate, and now in love calls me to share in His sufferings?

Now I understand love. Now I know love. Now I've experienced love. Love is patient, love is kind. It does not envy; it does not boast; it is not proud. It is not rude; it is not self-seeking; it is not easily angered; it keeps no record of wrongs. Love does not delight in evil but rejoices with the truth. It always protects, always trusts, always hopes, always perseveres. Love never fails.

How shall I respond to love? By serving the One I love, and the ones He loves. It is an honor that I don't deserve, chief of sinners though I am. But I will gladly, expectantly, suffer for the sake of the name of Jesus, and the loving relationship He started with me through my experience. How about you?

– Based on Acts 8:3; Acts 9:1-19; 1 Corinthians 13:1-8; Galatians 1:13-14; Philippians 3:4-6; 1 Timothy 1:15

Is Christianity, at its core, about believing in God, or is it about knowing God? Is it about giving intellectual ascent to the right doctrine, or is it about having a real relationship with the Creator of the universe?

The apostle Paul, whose conversion experience is dramatized above, was all about right doctrine. He wrote most of the New Testament for us through the inspiration of the Holy Spirit and thereby codified most of our doctrine. Good doctrine is important.

Paul had continual experiences with God, coming out of his relationship with him. He was an example of the balance we should be trying to strike. He longed to know God, not just about him. He sums it up in Philippians 3:8-11:

I consider everything a loss compared to the surpassing of knowing Christ Jesus my Lord, for whose sake I have lost all things. I consider them rubbish, that I may gain Christ and be found in him, not having a righteousness of my own that comes from the law, but that which is through faith in Christ—the righteousness that comes from God and is by faith. I want to know Christ and the power of his resurrection and the fellowship of sharing in his sufferings, becoming like him in his death, and so, somehow, to attain the resurrection from the dead (Philippians 3:8-11).

Certainly Christianity includes a belief system, and there are certain tenets we must ascribe to if we're going to call ourselves Christians. But if that's all Christianity is to us, then experience is not required. We could go to church every Sunday, give our mental ascent to what the pastor said as truth, and then live out the rest of the week however we wanted. In this scenario, God is not real to us. Why? Because we haven't experienced Him in our life; we've only believed things about Him.

What did Jesus say in John 10:10? "I have come that they might have perfect doctrine and have it to the full." Nope. "I have come that they might finally understand predestination vs. free will." Wrong again. It was, "I have come that they might have life, and have it to the full."

Guess what? Life is an experience. To live life to the full

is to experience much. Think back to the illustration about my daughter and me and the swings. Which one of us knows swings better? My little daughter, who has experienced swings, knows swings better than me, the engineer who knows all about swings. I believe swings should be fun. But she knows swings are fun because she's experienced a swing.

The essence of Christianity is life experience with and of God, not intellectual ascent to certain truths about him. Even the demons know all the perfect doctrine about God, but it does them no good (James 2:19).

God is known, like anyone else, through our experience of him. If we never experience God and hence, never know Him, aren't we likely to hear Him say on that great and terrible day of the Lord (Joel 2:31) when He returns, "I never knew you. Away from me, you evildoers" (Matthew 7:23)?

But why does it have to be emotional and messy? Because we're emotional and messy. It won't be emotional and messy all the time, but it will be sometimes, and at God's choosing, not ours. Jesus wants to be the Lord of our entire being, not shut out of our emotions or any other part of us. He wants to sit on the throne over our whole self, not just the parts we feel safe letting Him have and letting others see.

Experience with God is absolutely necessary, not for salvation, but to know Him and the fullness of all He has for us. But, as necessary as experience with Him is, the experience in and of itself is incomplete—not an end in itself.

A dying man in the desert needs water, but he needs the container also, or the water slips through his fingers into the sand and is wasted. In the same way, we desperately need the fresh, life-giving water of experience with God in our lives. But we need to steward it rightly.

Really Knowing

We need to prayerfully search out and intentionally pursue the interpretation, application/wisdom, and timing. And we need this whole process to be pastored by our pastor. There's a point to our experience; God gave it for a reason. He's doing something in our lives. And He's wanting us and waiting for us and longing for us to seek Him out to find out what it is.

We should be longing for Him, the one we love, not the experience or the fireworks—that will happen all on its own without our help, as long as we don't resist it.

Experience with God is not the fullness of all He has for us, but it is the vehicle for getting there—a rich, personal relationship with Him.

So we should be free to experience God in our churches. And we should be open to our pastor as he guides, directs, teaches, and pastors us through the experiences into the interpretation of what they mean, the application/wisdom of how they apply to our lives, what to do about them, and the timing of when to do it.

We shouldn't judge other people's experiences or make our experiences a doctrine to impose on anyone else. And we shouldn't go on and on gushing about our experience. We should go on and on gushing about Jesus—the one we love.

Jesus is the point. He's the end in Himself. It's all about Him.

About the Author

Author and speaker Dave Wernli grew up with a solid, evangelical, biblical foundation in Southern California, active in Lutheran and Evangelical Free churches. A software engineer for more than twenty-five years, God crashed in on his nice, neat, analytical world and flipped it upside down. Spending time in the Vineyard and Foursquare churches and the Prayer Movement, Dave has learned about the Holy Spirit and deeply loves both the evangelical and charismatic traditions, considering himself a child of both. He currently lives in Virginia with his wife and children.

Please check his blog at www.davewernli.com, where he writes about our true identity in Christ and knowing Jesus as our Lover-King. To schedule speaking engagements, please send email to schedule@davewernli.com.